# PETER

## THE GRACE OF NEW BEGINNINGS

SAM CHESS

**PETER – THE GRACE OF NEW BEGINNINGS**



Published by:

PANTHERA PUBLISHING
PANTHERAPUBLISHING.COM
STUART, FLORIDA



First Printing – December 2023
Printed in the United States of America

 *(There is a comprehensive Scripture index at the end of the book, with additional versions used with permission.)*

Cover picture background: "Designed by brgfx / Freepik," and arranged by Penny Worley

ISBN 978-0-9997977-7-8

# Table of Contents

# Introduction

---

*Please don't skip the introduction!*
*It sets the stage for Peter's life.*

The subtitle of this book about Peter is *The Grace of NEW Beginnings*. Those key words are so significant in Peter's life, and they're supposed to be in our lives too. That little word NEW fills the pages of Scripture. Notice this famous passage in the next to last chapter of the Bible:

> **Revelation 21:1-5: "Then I saw a new heaven and a new earth, for the old heaven and the old earth had disappeared.** *(This is just as time as we know it comes to an end, and our eternity with God begins.)* **And I saw the holy city, the New Jerusalem, coming down from God out of Heaven like a bride beautifully dressed for her husband. I heard a loud shout from the throne, saying, 'Look, God's home is now among his people! He will live with them, and they will be his people. God himself will be with them. He will wipe every tear from their eyes, and there will be no more death or sorrow or crying or pain. All these things are gone forever.' And the one sitting on the throne said, 'Look, I am making everything new!'"**

*Behold I am making everything NEW!*

Do you see that re-occurring word that grabs our attention! NEW Heavens, NEW Earth, NEW Jerusalem. Then God caps it all off with "I'm going to just go ahead and make every-thing NEW!" There is something deep inside many/all of us that screams – "Yes, that's what we are looking for! That's what we all so need!" When we look at the world around us and then read, **"He will wipe every tear from our eyes, and there will be no more death or sorrow or crying or pain,"** we scream "Yes" from the depths of our soul! The reason the word NEW is so appealing is because the old sin-cursed world around us is often so unappealing!

I got curious about the word "new" in Scripture and pulled out every use of the word in the whole Bible. *(It's used over 500 times.)* I ended up with 86 pages of Scripture and context. Here's what I discovered:

- The theology of "New" really is a big deal in the Bible almost certainly because Genesis starts out with humanity rebelling against their loving Creator and falling into unfixable sin. We humans desperately needed a way out of the effects of satan's curse.
- God graciously unfolds the pathway to forgiveness and righteousness. God himself arrived on this planet, and squeezed into a human baby embryo, so he could die to pay our un-payable sin penalty!

What is compelling to me is how many times God attaches the word NEW to that unfolding Gospel story. The Greek word for "Gospel" literally means "Good News." The English word news has the word new in it, on purpose. We often see the word "Gospel" or "Good News" as kind of a catch-all, filler word, but it isn't, not to God! It is an important theological concept that God wants to bury in all of our brains.

The Old Testament starts out with lots of "new" references like new year, new harvest, new moon festival, new wine-skins which seem to describe events going on "outside of a person's soul." But when you carefully line up all the Old Testament references chronologically, you can literally watch the change that begins to unfold in David's Psalms and in Ezekiel and Isaiah – when phrases like "a new song, a new heart, a new spirit, a new Covenant begin to show up."

The word "new" starts to be attached to what God wants to do in our soul! When we get into the written new Covenant *(or the New Testament)* this snowballing word "new" explodes open in the pages of Scripture.

> **2 Corinthians 5:17 NIV: "Therefore, if anyone is in Christ, that person is a new creation! The old has gone, the new is here! "**
>
> **Hebrews 10:19-22: "We can boldly enter Heaven's Most Holy Place because of the blood of Jesus. By his death, Jesus opened a new and life-giving way through the curtain into the Most Holy Place.** *(Visualize the curtain splitting – into the direct presence of God)* **And since we have a great High Priest** *(Jesus)* **who rules over God's house, let us go right into the presence of God with sincere hearts fully trusting him!"**

You can quickly see how God's promises to give the straying Children of Israel "a new spirit and a new heart" has opened up into something much, much bigger as this theology of "newness" increasingly unfolds in the Bible. When God first promises "newness" halfway into the Old Testament, the ancients are kind of shocked! Very little, to them, was ever "new." Spiritually, things seemed to stay the same century after century!

Then dramatic change arrived, as they discovered that God had a plan to transform them from the inside out. And it wasn't going to be based on how many sacrifices they could bring. God was promising to make them into entirely new people, not because of something they manufactured from within or some set of rules they kept on the outside. God was promising to take the old away and replace it with the spiritually brand new by the power of his indwelling Holy Spirit. Watch this barrage from Paul's Epistle to the Romans:

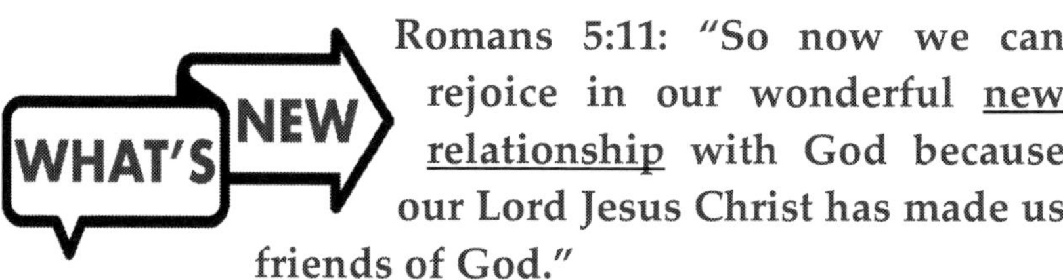


**Romans 5:11: "So now we can rejoice in our wonderful new relationship with God because our Lord Jesus Christ has made us friends of God."**

**Romans 5:18: "Yes, Adam's one sin brings condemnation for everyone, but Christ's one act of righteousness brings a right relationship with God and new life for everyone."**

> Romans 6:4: **"For we died and were buried with Christ by baptism. And just as Christ was raised from the dead by the glorious power of the Father, now <u>we also may live new lives</u>."**
>
> Romans 12:2: **"Don't copy the behavior and customs of this world, but let God <u>transform you into a new person by changing the way you think</u>."**

So, here is where this book is headed. I thought: If only there was somebody in Scripture that could be a perfect example of this new life unfolding? If only there was somebody we could study that would let us look deep into his/her sinfulness and then let us visually see the transforming power of God at work!

- If only we could get "before, after, and during" high definition "inspired-Scripture" snapshots into someone who came to **"belong to Christ and <u>became a new person. The old was gone, the new had come!</u>"**
- You say, "Sam there are scores of people, in the Bible who were very sinful, but who became pictures of God's powerful grace!" Yes, that's true, but so often we are given a "before snapshot" and an "after snapshot," without many "in between shots" turning those photos into an unfolding "movie" in our brains.

For instance, the Philippian Jailer who held Paul and Silas in the Roman out-colony of Philippi. Philippi had the same sexually-perverted, human-sacrificing religion that we often associate with Ephesus or Corinth. The Jailer had very possibly sacrificed one of his own children to the idol Molech. They all were required to. After the earthquake, Mr. Jailer and his whole household were saved! And just 12 years later Paul writes the "book" of Philippians back to that church and addresses them as the "Saints in Philippi" – one of whom would have almost certainly been that former human-sacrificing Jailer!

- From blood-spilling pervert to "Saint," in just 12 years! That's amazing! That's the power of God's grace!
- But, we don't have any snapshots in the middle to show us Mr. Jailer's progression from Sinner to Saint! If only we had somebody, in Scripture, we could study deeply all along the way! Well, what do you know – God saw fit to give us just such an example!

There is one person's life in the New Testament that we are allowed to look deeply into – from the time he begins to follow Jesus until just before his martyred death. We get to vividly see the sin spilling out all over him, and then we get to read words he wrote that are now part of inspired Scripture that literally guide our spiritual development almost 2000 years later.

**Paul – a Murderer Turned Apostle**

Sam, you must be talking about the Apostle Paul. The murderer of Christians turned Apostle to the whole world! What a change from an angry, vicious "defender of the Jewish faith" that drove him to kill what he saw as "blaspheming Christ- followers" to become one of the greatest Jesus-followers of all time who wrote 13 books in our New Testament!

No, he's a good example of soul-transformation, but I'm not writing about him! Why? Remember, from the time of Paul's conversion in Acts 9 *(AD 34)* until the time he starts his ministry in Acts 11 *(AD 47)*, we don't get to see inside those developing years of the Apostle Paul. *(That's 14 silent years!)*

- We don't get to know what struggles he had; we don't see what sins tripped him up.
- We don't know what he had to confess, perhaps over and over, until real transformation took hold.
- We know he was a man with a vicious anger. How long was it before that anger was transformed? We don't know.

Paul never even physically met Jesus face to face except as " a light and a voice" from Heaven on the road to Damascus. Whatever convictions Jesus spoke into his life, we aren't able to hear and study them. But <u>there is somebody else</u>, where we are able to dissect conversation after conversation. We get to see the open sin; hear the convicting words; and internalize the intense repentance.

1) Next to Jesus this person is mentioned more times, by name, in the New Testament than any other

person. *(Jesus name is used 1538 times. Paul's name is mentioned 156 times. This person's name is mentioned 160 times.)*

2) This "disciple" spoke more often and had more of his direct spoken words recorded in the New Testament than any of the other disciples.

3) This disciple was spoken directly to, by Jesus, more than any other disciple.

4) No disciple was ever honored more directly and more profoundly by Jesus than this disciple.

5) Yet, no disciple, no follower of Jesus was more sharply rebuked and reproved than this person.

6) No one ever claimed such great loyalty to Jesus outspokenly acknowledging his Lordship; and then so completely denied and rejected Jesus!

The answer to all the above descriptions is *(as our title suggests)* **Peter!** Peter is always the first name in the four Gospel listings of the disciples. The question we should probably all be asking is "Why"?

Andrew, Peter's brother and fishing partner, was older and much more steady and sane. But he's not mentioned all that much. Instead, at the top of each of the four 'disciple lists' in the Gospels are Peter, James and John. James and John's nickname was "the sons of thunder" *(undoubtedly for good reason),* and Peter seems to be the most unstable "first choice" Jesus could have possibly picked!

Had we lived in the first century, we would have questioned all of Jesus' choices for disciples. They were all Galileans except for traitor Judas who was from a little town called Kerioth in the south. Galileans were rural people, country-folk, "knuckle-draggers," not part of the elite like the snooty people down in Jerusalem. None were part of the nobility, none were Pharisees, none were Sadducees *(the learned people in society),* none were scribes, nobody was prominent or wealthy, they all were dirty blue collar workmen except Matthew who was a "traitorous to the Jews" tax collector for Rome. Four were fishermen. One was a terrorist! *(Literally)* Simon the Zealot!

The Zealots hated Rome and wanted the Empire overthrown. They were often called "sicarri," because they carried a little sword called a "sicae." They would sneak up behind a Roman, at night, stab him in the back and slip away. They were "domestic terrorists"!

What was Jesus thinking? A terrorist among his disciples? Can you imagine how disciple Matthew *(the tax collector for Rome)* was always looking over his shoulder whenever disciple Simon came up behind him?

But forget Judas the Traitor and Simon the Zealot for now. They are not the focus of this book. Peter is!

# Chapter 1

*Peter – The arrogant big mouth!*

---

Why would Jesus make Simon Peter his main storyline? Why would there be more information about Peter; more conversations by him; and more conversations directed to him than any other person in the whole New Testament? Peter's reputation was as a big-mouth screw-up!

Years later, when Peter was seasoned by his failures and had thoroughly repented, he would write letters now called 1 and 2 Peter in your Bible. He would write these verses many of us have probably memorized:

> **1 Peter 5:5-6NIV: "All of you clothe yourselves with humility toward one another, because, 'God opposes the proud but gives grace to the humble.' Humble yourselves, therefore, under God's mighty hand, that he may lift you up in due time."**

The man who wrote those verses *(about AD 62)* 34 years earlier, when he was a rookie disciple of Jesus, was one of the least humble people on the planet! When Jesus chose him, and during the first three years when he was a disciple of Jesus, Peter was anything but "clothed in humility"!

- He was extremely arrogant! He had a massively big untamed mouth! He could not seem to "humble himself under God's mighty hand," no matter how hard he tried!
- He didn't need God to "lift him up." He was busy 24 hours a day lifting himself up!

The amazing point is Jesus not only chose him as his first disciple, but seemed intent on spelling out for all of us who would follow all the "wise-guy" things that Peter said, all the arrogant responses: and all the falling-on-his-face failures. Then in a logic that we struggle to understand, Jesus takes the least likely person and lifts him to the number one place in leadership in his newly forming Church! Why?

**A Closed Mouth Gathers No Feet**

Why would Jesus do that? I'm sure there were several other disciples who were more mature and much less arrogant. Doesn't it seem like God would want to give us more wise words from somebody who didn't always have at least one foot jammed in his mouth? How can we even understand someone who is always talking through his toes?

Why? Why would Jesus want Peter as his main storyline? Because that's who the greatest number of us can relate to! Most of us tend to be arrogant, to one degree or another. It's part of the human condition. We focus on our own needs and wants from the time we are a tiny infant.

*"I spend a great chunk of my life, realizing I should have shut up ten minutes ago!"*

Some of us have big uncontrollable mouths! Most of us know what it means to have our foot in our mouth, more than we want to admit. Most of us know exactly what it means to fail God and those around us way too often.

So God uses an in-your-face, big-mouthed screw up who eventually became the most powerful, righteous voice of the Early Church – to show us just how far he can, and will, bring each of us if we are willing! From a man who denied he even knew Jesus just before Jesus' crucifixion: a man who would eventually also be crucified: he would ask to be crucified upside down *(tradition says)* because he thought he didn't deserve to be martyred just like his Lord!

---

There are many things I want to highlight in the following chapters *(that have become amazing new truths to me in preparation for this book)*. Let me first hit some familiar highlights that let us look directly into Peter's soul and see some amazing interactions between him and Jesus.

Let's join Jesus and Peter at the Last Supper where Jesus washes the disciple's feet *(including Judas who would soon betray him, and Simon the terrorist – being careful not to brush against his dagger)*. When he reaches Simon Peter, what comes out of Peter's mouth is "classic Simon."

*A footnote*: Most of us know that Jesus himself would change Peter's name from Simon *(a reed – a whistling sound)* to Peter *(Petros-rock).* I've preached whole sermons about how Jesus can take the reed swaying/whistling in the wind and turn it into a granite cliff of strength. *(The root of the word Simon also means "flat nose." Maybe that is significant from him running into a wall a little too often?)*

But it never occurred to me that even after Peter makes enough spiritual progress that Jesus *(prophetically)* gives him the new name "Rock," – Jesus himself doesn't always call him Peter! When he is trying to challenge him to move toward the man he is going to become, Jesus often calls him Peter the Rock.

- When Peter is seemingly stumbling around in the dark, Jesus sometimes refers back to his untransformed name Simon. *(a reed blowing in the wind.)*
- Sometimes when Peter has his foot crammed clear back in his mouth. Jesus even doubles his old name up and says: "Simon, Simon"!
- But Jesus is never doing it to mock him. Jesus always, always wants Simon Peter's best eternal good – and the same is true for every one of us!

If Jesus didn't have any place in his kingdom for fumbling, stumbling, faulted people, he wouldn't have gone to so much effort to highlight Simon Peter. If Jesus didn't have any place in his kingdom for fumbling, stumbling, faulted people, he wouldn't end up with any kingdom at all because most of the "Saints" he is building his kingdom with are a lot like Peter*!* *(Watch this.)*

> **John 13:6-9: : "When Jesus came to Simon Peter, Peter said to him, 'Lord, are you going to wash my feet?'** *(Yes Simon, you may have noticed – I am washing everyone's feet)* **Jesus replied, 'You don't understand now what I am doing, but someday you will.' '<u>No</u>,' Peter protested, <u>you will never ever wash my feet</u>!' Jesus replied, 'Unless I wash you, you won't belong to me.' Simon Peter exclaimed, 'Then wash my hands and head as well, Lord, not just my feet!'"**

*Classic Peter!* "You're not going to try this servant stuff on me too are you, Jesus? I'm Peter! Why are you embarrassing us both by kneeling in front of me? You will <u>never ever wash my feet</u>!"

*Classic Jesus:* "If you refuse to let me wash your feet, you are publicly declaring your independence from my will? Is that what you want to do, Peter?"

*Transforming Peter:* "No, my no! I was just running off at the mouth, with my brain in neutral as usual, Lord! Why don't you just dump the whole rest of the bowl over me! <u>LORD</u>!" *(v: 9)*

Does anybody else (*other than me)* not relate to Peter at this point? We miss entirely what God is trying to do in our lives because we are so sure and so intent that he should be going about it in another way! When Jesus finally breaks into our stubborn minds with the great grace he is longing to pour in and through our lives, we are so taken aback we say *(or think),* "Jesus, just hold up your foot washing bowl – I'll jam my whole face in it"!

Finally, Peter gets to take part in the Last Supper and hears Jesus explain his coming death and how the elements of the meal are reminders of his *(coming)* broken body and spilled-out blood. It's a solemn and holy moment! But, *(Can you believe it?)* the next thing you hear in the quiet somber atmosphere of the Last Supper are *(again)* Jesus' voice and one other raised voice. Would you like to guess whose voice is once again rising above the rest – the center of the next outburst?

> **John 13:33, 36-37NIV:"My children, I will be with you only a little longer. You will look for me, and just as I told the Jews, so I tell you now: Where I am going, you cannot come.' Simon Peter asked him, 'Lord, where are you going?' Jesus replied, 'Where I am going, you cannot follow now, but you will follow me later.' Peter asked, 'Lord, why can't I follow you now? I will lay down my life for you.'"**

*Classic Peter:* He could have perhaps added something like, "You've said three times so far that you are going to die. You've also said that you are 'going to rise again,' whatever that means. I don't have any intention of letting you die to start with." *(He'll prove that a few hours later by pulling his sword and chopping off Malchus' ear.)* "But if they do manage to get through my 'wall of steel' Jesus, I promise that I will be right there beside you! If they run you through with a sword, it better be a long sword, because they are going to have to run it through me too"!

*Jesus:* "No, Peter no! You're still all arrogant talk. You are not yet really sold out to follow me! Someday you will be! Some-day you will follow me into martyrdom, but not today! Today you will run away like a scared rabbit."

> **John 13:38NIV: "Then Jesus answered, 'Will you really lay down your life for me? I tell you the truth, before the rooster crows, you will disown me three times'"!** "Not a chance, Jesus. Not a chance. You get most things right, but this one you got completely wrong!" *Luke records:*
>
> **Luke 22:31-34NIV: "'Simon, Simon, Satan has asked to sift you as wheat. But I have prayed for you, Simon, that your faith may not fail. And when you have turned back, strengthen your brothers.' But he replied, 'Lord, I am ready to go with you to prison and to death.' Jesus answered, 'I tell you, Peter, before the rooster crows today, you will deny three times that you know me.'"**

- Peter, you are going to stumble badly. I'm praying that your faith won't fail completely.
- I already know it won't because… **"when you have turned back,"** and you will, when you have smacked into the ground; and slowly climbed back up; and wiped off the mud then,
- **"Strengthen your brothers"!** Peter – with all your stubborn faults, I'm still counting on you to lead!

It actually did turn out to be a great evening. After the meal, the Bible says they moseyed out toward the Mount of Olives. Mark 14 says they sang hymns. Jesus taught them amazing truths found in John 14-17. But can't you just hear Peter, throughout the evening, leaning over to one disciple after another saying, "Did you hear what Jesus said to me back there? Maybe if he had been talking about one of the rest of you, it would have been more believable, but – I'm Peter!"

*For I know the plans I have for you, declares the Lord! (Jeremiah 29:11)*

1) If Peter had "really believed" Jeremiah's prophesy – that Jesus had complete knowledge of every moment of every one of his days and was moving ahead of him to clear the path, Peter would not have spent so much time fighting God's plan for his life!

2) If we "really believed" Jeremiah's prophesy that Jesus has complete knowledge of every moment of every one of our days and is moving ahead of us to clear the path, we would not spend so much time fighting God's plan for our lives!

Finally, they all arrive at the Garden of Gethsemane. Jesus chooses *(of all people)* Peter… and James and John *(the Sons of Thunder)* to "watch with him" as he prays before his death. But Peter, full of food and self-assurance, sleeps like a baby as Jesus' great spiritual battle rages. Jesus didn't really take Peter into the Garden to "pray for him" and what he was getting ready to endure. He took him into the Garden to learn to "resist satan's attacks" in his own life! Peter's lack of attentiveness was not going to make one drop of difference in what was going to happen to Jesus in the next three days, but it would play heavily on Peter's future failures.

Peter was full of ear-chopping adrenaline when the soldiers came into the Garden, but then it seems like all his surge of intensity oozed away. **Luke 22:54-57: "So they arrested him** *(Jesus)* **and led him to the high priest's home. And Peter followed at a distance. The guards lit a fire in the middle of the courtyard and sat around it, and Peter joined them there. A servant girl noticed him in the firelight and began staring at him. Finally she said, 'This man was one of Jesus' followers!' But Peter denied it. 'Woman,' he said, 'I don't even know him'"!**

What kind of confusion must have been going on inside Peter's head? Where's the brash arrogance now? Where's the self-assurance? He didn't even keep up with the crowd of crucifiers, and a servant girl's question has him running like a scared rodent!

> **Luke 22:58-60: "After a while someone else looked at him and said, 'You must be one of them!' 'No, man, I'm not!' Peter retorted. About an hour later someone else insisted, 'This must be one of them, because he is a Galilean, too.' But Peter said, 'Man, I don't know what you are talking about.' And immediately, while he was still speaking, the rooster crowed."**

I want us to carefully notice the next words, because they tell us so much about Jesus, **Luke 22:61: "At that moment <u>the Lord turned and looked at Peter</u>. Suddenly, the Lord's words flashed through Peter's mind: 'Before the rooster crows tomorrow morning, you will deny three times that you even know me.'"** What do you think was in that look? Anger? Betrayal? No chance! No way!

Jesus, with all the chaos and trauma going on in his life knew exactly where Peter was in that court-yard! Peter had not resisted temptation! Jesus, well out of earshot, had heard every one of Peter's denials. He felt every one of Peter's fears. His love for Peter was overwhelming and his only goal for wayward Peter was forgiveness, restoration, and turning him into a burning spiritual firestorm! You can count on the fact that Jesus look was not one of condemnation! It was a look of compassion, of assurance.

- That rooster crowing at that time of the night was no freak accident. Why was rooster crowing at night? Why just one?
- Roosters seldom crow at night. So why? Because Jesus nodded at the rooster, and said crow! It was perfectly timed. It was a personal message from Jesus to Peter. There was nothing in the crow that said "I hate you, you filthy deny-er"!
- What was in that single "crow" was Jesus' reminder, from the evening before that he would forgive and completely restore Peter.

**Luke 22:61: "At that moment the Lord turned and looked at Peter. Suddenly, the Lord's words flashed through Peter's mind."** Peter remembered! This is not a postscript – this is important! There is no question that Peter's life turned radically around that day! The crowing rooster that Jesus ordered to crow that night, was not crowing, "You're a failure!" It was crowing a message of "New Beginnings"!

- What is actually the role of a crowing rooster? He almost always heralds the coming of a new day!
- Peter may have been swamped by shame and conviction, but he did indeed get the message of "new beginnings."
- That famous rooster may have uncharacteristically "beat the sun" by a few hours, but his message came through loud and clear; there still was compassion and forgiveness for Peter if he would just repent and truly follow Jesus!

Three days later Peter is rushing to an empty tomb! He gets a personal message delivered *(by way of the women)* right from the angels, to him:

*"Tell his disciples and Peter"!*

**Mark 16:7NIV: "Go, tell his disciples AND PETER,** *(Jesus has risen!)* **'He is going ahead of you into Galilee. There you will see him, just as he told you.'"** *(Make sure you get every bit of that message to Peter!)*

Peter will spend part of 40 glorious days basking in the presence of the risen, living and loving Jesus who has so completely forgiven him, who has an amazing plan for Peter's life! But Peter is not ready for that "amazing plan" quite yet…

# Chapter 2

*"Peter, do you really love me?"*

---

We started in the introduction of this book with the subject of what it means to have new life in Christ Jesus! If you come into a church, on a Sunday morning, with all kinds of sinful habits, actions, reactions, and attitudes – and I, or some other pastor, teacher, or spiritual leader tell you that you can confess those sinful actions and Jesus will forgive you – but unfortunately you are stuck with who you are, and there is just no possibility of life change or spiritual transformation

- If I, or any pastor were to tell you that there is no possibility of "leaving the old sinful you behind and taking on a new righteous you."
- If that what anyone teaches you – you should walk back out the door and find a place with better spiritual answers – because that is not what the Bible promises!

> **2 Corinthians 5:17: "Therefore, if anyone is in Christ, that person is a new creation! The old has gone, the new has come!"**
>
> Romans 12:2: **"Don't copy the behavior and customs of this world, but let God transform you into a new person by changing the way you think."**

So, we set out to find somebody who could be a high-definition mental movie of that kind of transformation, and we sure found him – Peter! Amazingly, we are allowed to look behind the curtain into Peter's life and actually see the promised transformation taking place! We have just begun our journey of seeing Simon's raw sinfulness being changed into a brand-new righteous person who will eventually have a huge impact on the whole world for Jesus' Kingdom.

This picture is not really Peter. This is how I picture him. He was a tough guy. He wasn't a lawyer or a sandal salesman. He was a commercial fisherman.

We used to have four families of commercial fishermen in our church before a new net ban law forced them out of our state. I went out fishing with them, they were tough, tough guys! Their attitude was a lot like gold prospectors. One week they would haul in thousands of pounds of fish and make a killing. The next five weeks they would hardly make enough money for gas – but that next big haul always drove them back out. That was Peter *(and Andrew, James and John)*. It is interesting to me that five of the most profound books in your Bible were eventually written by two of those tough guys!

Peter wasn't just tough-as-nails. As we have noted, he was a proud, arrogant, big-mouth bully. He had a huge untamed mouth! As we also noted, 32 years later tough-guy Peter would write, "Humble yourself under the mighty hand of God"! But early on in Simon Peter's discipleship, he could not seem to humble "himself under God's mighty hand," no matter how hard he tried! He was constantly talking over top of Jesus, contradicting him, telling Jesus he didn't know what he was talking about. Yet, he is the disciple who when Jesus eventually asked him to acknowledge out-loud, who he believed Jesus actually was – he would scream out, "You are the Christ *(the Messiah)* the Son of the Living God"!

- Just six months after that amazing confession, after having watched Jesus heal thousands of sick people and raise three dead people back to life,
- After watching Jesus walk on top of the raging sea and invite him to walk toward him – after seeing a few loaves and fish turned into a massive banquet twice!
- And after seeing a four-day, rotting dead man, *(their mutual friend Lazarus)* raised back to life,

After all that, just six months after Peter declares that he knew Jesus to be "the Messiah, the Son of the Living God," we found him huddled beside a campfire denying that they'd ever met! That's Peter! So many people, in our church have said to me, "I see my own life reflected in this guy." I do too! That's the whole point! We noticed earlier: No disciple was ever honored more directly and more intensely by Jesus than Peter, and yet no disciple was ever more sharply rebuked for his bad behavior than Peter. Many of us reading this book can almost certainly relate to that! The writer can too! Sometimes we are spiritually doing so well, walking arm-in-arm with the Creator of the Universe. And then *(bam)* we find ourselves face-planted in the dirt of our sinful nature, and we wonder if Jesus will turn and walk away from us shaking his head in disgust.

NO! That's another whole point of this high-definition movie of Peter's life! Jesus has zero interest in beating us down! He has a massive "universe-sized interest" in lifting us up to become what we could never have become on our own!

That's why he left Heaven and came to this earth to pay our sin penalty! That blood-spilling, crucified Jesus is not a Savior who is interested in smashing you into the dirt! Picture Jesus hanging on the cross with his loving arms of forgiveness open wide toward you! He's not even one bit interested in anybody's failure! Jesus wants nothing but our unlimited eternal success!

> Remember this vivid picture: **Luke 22:61: "At that moment** *(his three denials)* **the Lord turned and looked at Peter. Suddenly, the Lord's words flashed through Peter's mind: 'Before the rooster crows tomorrow morning, you will deny three times that you even know me.'"**

Jesus heard every one of Peter's denials. He felt every single one of Peter's fears. His love for Peter was overwhelming and his only goal for wayward, proud Peter was forgiveness and restoration. You can count on the fact that Jesus' look was a look of compassion, love, grace, forgiveness, and assurance. Peter failed Jesus *(and failed him, and failed him)*, but Jesus kept restoring, and restoring until Peter became one of the greatest Christian leaders on record and ended up writing two amazing epistles/letters in our New Testament.

Thirty-two years after Jesus' crucifixion, the tough old fisherman with a Holy Spirit infused mind and lots of new amazing life experiences is sitting at a desk putting the thoughts that are tumbling out of his brain onto paper.

He's not writing <u>at</u> the people who will read his letters *(that we now call 1 and 2 Peter in our Bible)*. He is undoubtedly thinking of the transformation that has taken place in his life and writing in awe, maybe with tears running down his still-grizzled face, as he thinks of the person he used to be!

- He had no idea that millions/billions of people would one day read his scrawled words. He didn't know people on the other side of the globe would drive to an "iron or concrete building" in "self-propelled movable metal machines" with steering wheels, and study his words 1,950 years later. *(It had only been 300 years since a Greek scientist even suggested that the world was round.)*

- But the words Peter scrawled one day under the inspiration of the Holy Spirit have become one of my own favorite passages in the whole Bible.

**2 Peter 1:3-4: "By his divine power, God has given us everything we need for living a godly life. We have received all of this by coming to know him, the one who called us to himself by means of his marvelous glory and excellence. And because of his glory and excellence, he has given us great and precious promises. These are the promises that enable you to share his divine nature and escape the world's corruption caused by human desires."**

Think about the emotions Peter must have been feeling as he wrote those words. What had happened in Peter's soul between him spitting out the words: **"Woman, I don't know what you are talking about,"** and him writing these words more than three decades later; **"Jesus' promises enable me to share in his divine nature"?**

The disciples were despondent after Jesus' crucifixion. Peter slinks off *(apparently)* by himself. Why would he not go with the other disciples? Because he had just made a complete idiot out of himself! Once again promising Jesus *(and all of the other disciples),* the moon and then delivering zip! The other ten disciples huddled together without Peter in blackness of mind. Why do you say, "without Peter," Sam? Because when the women arrived three days later and found the tomb empty, two angels told the women:

> **Mark 16:7 NIV: "Go, tell his disciples and Peter, *that Jesus has risen!* He is going ahead of you into Galilee. There you will see him, just as he told you."**

John chapter 20 records that he *(John)* and Peter both arrived at the tomb about the same time. Were they coming from the same place? Perhaps not! John, the young and spry, arrives, peeks inside the empty tomb, backs away and waits on the older Peter to huff and puff his way straight into the tomb door. John 20:8 says "John then went in, He saw and believed."

> **John 20:9-10, 19-20: "For until then they still hadn't understood the Scriptures that said Jesus must rise from the dead. Then they went home... That Sunday evening the disciples were meeting behind locked doors because they were afraid of the Jewish leaders. Suddenly, Jesus was standing there among them! 'Peace be with you,' he said... As he spoke, he showed them the wounds in his hands and his side. They were filled with joy when they saw the Lord!"**

Now the Disciples spiritual juices are, once again, flowing. Doubting Thomas, who said, "He wouldn't believe Jesus rose unless he put his fingers into the nail-prints in his hands" isn't there, so Jesus makes a second special appearance that includes him. These guys should have been on fire! Imagine all the meetings, all the planning sessions they needed to have. There's a worldwide church to build around this new truth of Jesus' death and resurrection! But what actually comes next in Scripture?

CHAPTER 2

# *Closed! Gone Fishing!*

**John 21:1-3: "Later, Jesus appeared again to the disciples beside the Sea of Galilee. This is how it happened. Several of the disciples were there—Simon Peter, Thomas... Nathanael from Cana in Galilee, the sons of Zebedee, and two other disciples. Simon Peter said, 'I'm going fishing.' 'We'll come, too,' they all said. So they went out in the boat, but they caught nothing all night."**

We should all be thinking: Say what? You're going to do what? You've just discovered that your Crucified Lord has risen from the dead. He's out there somewhere and instead of finding and asking him what the next plans for your life are, you're going where? To do what? You've got a whole world waiting to hear this new resurrection message and you're going out to catch fish?

Do you not remember that when Jesus called you to be his disciples he told you that you were no longer going to be catching fish but that you were going to become fishers of men? When exactly do you think that "fishers-of-men" task is supposed to kick in... Peter? Perhaps the recent death of Jesus to pay humanity's sin penalty and then his defeat of sin, and satan, and raising himself from the dead should be some kind of a clue?

Jesus, in his everlasting mercy and grace shows up beside the Sea of Galilee at dawn, and instead of telling them what unfaithful disciples they were – he fills their nets with a huge catch of fish. And when they finally all struggle *(with their 153 fish)* to the Sea's edge, Peter hops out of the boat *(again)* and swims through *(not on)* the water to Jesus. Jesus is there with a miraculously-made meal for his hungry fishermen friends. They sit down, across the fire from Jesus, just like old times.

Imagine how their frazzled minds began to settle. Not only had their crucified Lord risen from the dead – here they were sitting with him, just like old times, beside the Sea of Galilee. We're not told what conversation went on during the meal but you can just imagine the questions bubbling out of the disciples' mouths about what Jesus' death, and resurrection meant to them *(and to the whole world).*

- Perhaps Jesus even described to them what went on during those hours his body lay in the tomb. I've labored in sermons, over the Apostles' Creed statement, that Jesus descended into hell and took away the keys of death and of hell from satan! *(Revelation 1:18)*
- Tradition says that the Apostles' Creed was indeed written by the "Apostles." These are the very same faulted guys sitting by that campfire, early that morning, who would become future "Apostles."
- Wouldn't you have loved to have heard the bubbling questions these guys asked and the firsthand answers that they would have heard right from Jesus' mouth? Never again do we read: **"they still hadn't understood the Scriptures"!**
- But there is clearly tension in the air. Everyone was painfully aware that Peter, after swearing that if all

the other disciples forsook Jesus he never would – He then denied his Lord. He had sworn that if anybody tried to kill Jesus he would go to death with him. But when the soldiers hauled Jesus off for a mock trial, Peter was completely absent!

- He had denied/lied those famous three times that he ever knew Jesus! Peter was living with that fact hanging over his head every minute of every day, and he and everybody else knew it!

So, the lakeside, roasted-fish breakfast was over, and Jesus finally looked across the fire and centered his gaze on Peter. Everyone knew it was show-down time! Again, I suspect, in Jesus look that morning *(just like after Peter's denial),* there was not accusation, but compassion and restoration. We'll dissect every part of this short conversation *(because it's cram full of meaning),* but first let's read it.

**John 21:15-17 NIV: "When they had finished eating, Jesus said to Simon Peter, 'Simon son of John, do you truly love me more than these?' 'Yes, Lord,' he said, 'you know that I love you.' Jesus said, 'Feed my lambs.' Again Jesus said, 'Simon son of John, do you truly love me?' He answered, 'Yes, Lord, you know that I love you.' Jesus said, 'Take care of my sheep.' The third time he said to him, 'Simon son of John, do you love me?' Peter was hurt because Jesus asked him the third time, 'Do you love me?' He said, 'Lord, you know all things; you know that I love you.' Jesus said, 'Feed my sheep.'"**

What is Jesus up to here? Is he trying to embarrass Peter in front of his friends? No, of course not! Is Jesus trying to jab Peter publicly to make a point? NO! Jesus is getting ready to restore Peter, but it has to be public! And it is designed to make a point *(that will endure right up to us reading this book today)*. But it's not going to be a negative point. Some of what Jesus says to Peter does cut him deeply, but that's not the purpose! Jesus' purpose is going to be the final restoration of Peter into total forgiveness and back into a lifetime of ministry not just for his generation, but for 19+ centuries of generations to come.

By this time everybody knows about Peter's triple denial. It's been hanging over his head every day. Jesus public restoration is the kindest thing he could have done for Peter. Once it's over everyone will know that!

1) Jesus forgives Peter.
2) Jesus restores Peter.
3) Jesus wants Peter, even in spite of his faults, to be a leader in his new Church. In fact one of the greatest church leaders of all time! There is a lesson in that!

How many questions does Jesus ask Peter? Three! Why three? Why not two or five? Is Jesus stuttering? Is Peter like a scratched vinyl record, that just keeps playing the same notes over and over? NO! There were three questions because there were … 3 denials! Many people don't see this as a question for each of Peter's denials, but it almost certainly was. That's the way the ancient Middle Eastern mind worked.

And notice the setting, sitting around a campfire, not only eating but warming themselves after a miserably cold night on the Sea. When was the last time you saw Peter warming himself beside a campfire? At his denial of Jesus! Indeed! *(Now we are catching on!)* And these same thoughts were crashing into Peter's mind as well!

- Three times Peter denies Jesus as he warmed himself by a fire. Three times Jesus questions him over the breakfast fire.
- To my western "occidental" mind this might seem like just so much coincidence. To the Jews eastern "oriental minds" it was significant, very significant.

And every part of Jesus' questions has so much meaning. How does Jesus start the questioning? With Peter's name, of course, but look what name he uses: **John 21:15: "When they had finished eating, Jesus said to Simon Peter, "Simon son of John, do you truly love me more than these?"**

There really is a deep cut there, do you see it? Jesus calls Peter, "Simon," his original name. Jesus had told Peter he would no longer be called Simon; he would be known as Peter (Petros-rock), but here at this campfire setting, after his death and resurrection, he again calls Peter "a wind-blown reed." It was one more, hard reminder of Peter's self-centered arrogance. Jesus is calling him to finally put all of the "blowing in the wind Peter" behind him and move toward what his life was designed to become!

**John 21:15 NIV: "When they had finished eating, Jesus said to Simon Peter, '<u>Simon son of John, do you truly love me more than these</u>** (οὗτος - *houtos)***?'"**

<u>These</u>? T<u>hese what</u> – these other disciples? That would be an insensitive question. And how could Peter possibly know if his love was greater than anybody else in the group. Jesus had to be pointing at something. You don't say "these" unless you are specifying something. What could "these" have been? The firewood, the sand along the lake? What was "right there" that was unusual? <u>The huge catch of fish</u>! What did the huge catch of fish represent? Peter's self-sufficiency – the ability to do what he had learned to do best!

It's interesting *(to me)* that Jesus originally called Peter on the shore of this Sea of Galilee. Jesus re-commissioned Peter on the shore of the Sea of Galilee – and now he restores him from his three denials on the shore of the sea of Galilee! *(Each time, perhaps, within a few feet of each other?)* Peter, are you willing to put me ahead of all the things that give you security and comfort? Just how far are you willing to go, Peter, to give your whole life in an all-out, no-holds-barred submission to me? Here was the clincher question,

**"Simon son of John, do you truly love (**ἀγαπᾷς **) me more than these?"**

Here's a link you can't quite see in the English Bible. Jesus uses a word for love which means: "all-out, self-sacrificing, give-your-self away type of love."

Agape - *Agapao* – the same kind of love Jesus had for us, when he died for us! Peter, are you ready to return to me the kind of love I've just demonstrated to you?

*True or false:* Peter enthusiastically answers "Yes!" False! He waffles. **"Yes, Lord," he said, "you know that I love** (φιλῶ - *philo*)_**you." Jesus said, "Feed my lambs."** (ἀρνία- arnia – brand new little lambs)."

Again, what you can't see here in an English Bible is that Peter's response uses a different Greek word. His word for love (φιλῶ -*philo*) means that <u>he has a deep friendship with Jesus</u>, *(brotherly love).* Jesus, without blinking an eye, again commissions him to tend his Church after he's gone. *(A new church of newly "born-again" lambs.)*

Once again the same question comes from Jesus, but slightly modified. **V. 16: "Again Jesus said, 'Simon son of John, do you truly love (ἀγαπᾷς ) me?'** *Notice Jesus left off "more than these." He's now focusing purely on Peter's heart attitude.* **He answered, 'Yes, Lord, you know that I love *(φιλῶ - philo)* you.' Jesus said, 'Take care of my sheep'"** *(πρόβατον – more mature sheep, but easily led).*

I've been bothered in the past that Peter was not ready to make an all-out declaration of "agape" love. But the more that I looked at it this time, the more I thought, Peter is just being honest. He's saying the reality of what is in most of our hearts. Jesus is asking us for a radical commitment. Some of us have come to have a dear friend relationship with Jesus and that's not a bad thing – it's a good thing!

But Jesus is asking Peter for more! The truth is the process of moving from "acquaintance" to "real-vital-relationship" with our Savior – to an all-out self-sacrificing love relationship takes a lot of living and a lot of serving!

By the time Peter watches his friends and then his family around him being martyred, and then comes right up to a violent death by crucifixion himself – a lot of growth will have happened inside of him. The amazing thing is that Jesus was ready to use him way back in the very beginning even in his deeply faulted condition!

> So, on the final question Jesus slips back to the word Peter has been using and asks one more time: **John John 21:17 NIV: "The third time he said to him, 'Simon son of John, do you love** (φιλῶ - *philo*) **me?' Peter was hurt because Jesus asked him the third time, 'Do you love** (φιλῶ -*philo*) **me?' He said, 'Lord, you know all things; you know that I love** (φιλῶ - *philo*) **you.' Jesus said, 'Feed my sheep.'"**

This time Jesus is using the same word that Peter had used; "Are we friends? Are we really friends?" Peter is hurt because even though he hasn't been directly answering Jesus' "love" question, he has been assuring Jesus of his deep friendship.

And perhaps Jesus is saying. "It's Ok, Simon, I can work with that for now. What I want from you is for you to pour yourself into telling others the news of what I have done in your life. In turn, I will transform you into a man who truly "agapes" me with a self-sacrificing love, right up to giving your life in martyrdom for me!"

Let's face it, at some point in our lives, each of us may fail our Lord by giving into some temptation – sooner or later we could hear the "rooster crow." At that moment, the accusing voice of satan will ring in your mind telling you that you are finished, trying to please God is hopeless, your future has been destroyed! <u>But that is never God's message to you</u>! It doesn't matter who you are or what you have done, God is not just ready to forgive you, he is ready to transform you! And he is ready to reshape your life to be used in ways you could not have ever imagined. That's the message of Peter's life to each one of us today.

---

*Prayer:* Dear God, I am so much like Peter. I have been so arrogant and so self-sufficient. I confess to you today my stubborn self-sovereignty. I want to give my whole life in an all-out, no-holds-barred submission to you. If you can forgive a messed-up person like Peter, you can forgive a messed-up person like me. If you can transform and use an arrogant self-centered person like Peter, you can transform and use an arrogant self-centered person like me! I humble myself before you, my God, my Savior, and my Lord today – and I come running into your open, inviting arms of grace!

# Chapter 3

*Peter leaves behind his "self-directed" life!*

---

I did something while preparing this material that I had never done before. I pulled out every word that Peter said or wrote in the Bible after Jesus' resurrection and lined them up on 15 single-spaced pages. It's stunning to look in one setting at what came out of this guy's mouth, and from his pen, starting with his sermon on the Day of Pentecost up through the Epistles of 1 and 2 Peter – but my, what a mess he was to start with.

- No disciple is more publicly praised by Jesus for saying the right things and within a few hours more publicly rebuked than Peter. Jesus calls him satan, "get behind me satan"!
- No one ever claimed such loyalty to Jesus, and then nobody in all Scripture <u>so completely denied Jesus</u>!

And that event *(Peter's denial)* is kind of the fulcrum of Peter being yanked from the old bungling Peter and being remade into a new righteous Peter. Peter's greatest failure was his turning point, to become the most useful to God because *(and we all need to hear this)* <u>that is what God loves to do</u>!

*If anyone is in Christ, he is a new creation!*
*- 2 Corinthians 5:17*

That's the key for our study in this chapter. God took the least likely, the biggest jerk, the most messed-up man, and turned him into a mighty pillar of faith so that now millions of us study and live by his words.

*Let me show you this:* Remember it's only about 3 decades after his denial of Jesus that Peter starts writing inspired words like this in the opening paragraphs of 1 Peter.

> **1 Peter 1:13-16: "So prepare your minds for action and exercise self-control. Put all your hope in the gracious salvation that will come to you when Jesus Christ is revealed to the world. So you must live as God's obedient children. Don't slip back into your old ways of living to satisfy your own desires. You didn't know any better then. But now you must be holy in everything you do, just as God who chose you is holy. For the Scriptures say, 'You must be holy because I am holy.'"** *(Leviticus 11)*

Peter wrote that! "Constantly falling on his face" Peter! Completely lacking in self-control Peter! And I'm totally convinced that as he was writing it, he was undoubtedly overwhelmed by what a dip-wad he himself used to be!

**God does not call the qualified; He qualifies those who are called.**

But Jesus saw something in Peter that no-one else did! Jesus sees in us, what no one else often does! God so often chooses the least likely, the least qualified to accomplish the most eternal ends. He does not call the qualified, he qualifies the called!

Let's rewind again, then work our way back to where we are in studying Peter's life. I was intrigued by some new thoughts as I looked closely at all the words in the Bible describing Peter's transformation from least useful to most useful. Let me highlight Peter's "untransformed life" one more time.

- This is the guy who bragged loudly in front of the other disciples that if everyone else forsook Jesus he never would.
- This is the guy who when the Roman soldiers from Fort Antonia *(a contingent of 500 lived a few feet away)* came to carry out an arrest warrant on Jesus, along with the High Priest's goons, Peter, obviously had a "open-carry permit" for his sword. *(It's interesting that a fisherman from Galilee was walking around Jerusalem with a sword.)* Peter swishes it out and swings! He was not aiming at Malchus *(the servant of the High Priest)* ear – he intended to cut off his head right in front of dozens of seasoned soldiers.
- What did he think the outcome of that action would be? Answer: He didn't think at all! That was Peter, and me, and perhaps you! Peter appeared tough-as-nails right until this moment *(Watch the last sentence).*

***Luke 22:*61-62: "At that moment the Lord turned and looked at Peter, Suddenly, the Lord's words flashed through Peter's mind: 'Before the rooster crows tomorrow morning, you will deny three times that you even know me.' And Peter left the courtyard, weeping bitterly."** The seasoned, afraid-of-nothing businessman, who tried to hack an innocent servant's head off the day before in front of dozens of hardened soldiers, is sobbing his heart out because he finally realizes what a fraud he is! He goes off alone! Here is my take on the sequence of events:

1) Jesus is crucified! Peter goes off to "lick his wounds."

2) On Sunday morning, the women arrive and find an empty tomb.

3) They send word to the other disciples, and solitary, all alone, grieving Peter.

4) Peter and John arrive at the tomb about the same time and also find it empty.

5) Peter still doesn't go back and strategize with the other disciples. He again goes off to some lonely place to continue nursing his overwhelming grief.

6) How do we know that? Watch this. I'm not sure this has ever quite registered in my head.

We got some brief initial looks at Jesus' response to Peter's denial. There was the "compassionate look across the courtyard" of course, but Peter knew he was a traitor to Jesus! That is what he was thinking as he went off alone descending toward clinical depression. But was Jesus also branding him as a traitor? I imagine that the other disciples certainly were, and Peter knew it!

We can ask those same questions about ourselves. I ended the last chapter writing; "Some of us have heard the "rooster crowing" in our own lives, and like Peter, we might wonder if Jesus considers us a lost cause, a hopeless case, living life with a big "L" on our forehead? NO! Watch Jesus' actual responses to Peter. They tell us all we need to know.

#1) Jesus sent word through the angels to him:

**Mark 16:7 NIV: "But go, tell his disciples and** *(including)* **Peter, 'He is going ahead of you into Galilee. There you will see him, just as he told you.'"** I used this, in the last chapter, as an argument for why we know Peter was not holed up with the other disciples. But now notice this – far from Jesus considering Peter a traitor, a loser, a permanent failure – Jesus is going out of his way from the first post-resurrection communication to make sure that Peter knows he has not been cut off!

#2) Jesus met with him! *(This is a little bit of a shocker – to me.)*

They find Peter and tell him about the empty tomb. He takes off running: **Luke 24:14 NIV: "Peter, however, got up and ran to the tomb. Bending over, he saw the strips of linen lying by themselves, and he went away, wondering to himself what had happened."**

This next event is very important in our understanding of Peters' transformation. Jesus appears to two unnamed men on the road to Emmaus and "their hearts burned within them" at his words. *(He then went to their house, ate with them, and talked deeply with them vv. 30-31)* They finally realized they were talking to the risen Jesus, so they went rushing to the disciples with the news but watch these very revealing words.

> **Luke 24:32-34: "They said to each other, 'Didn't our hearts burn within us as he talked with us on the road and explained the Scriptures to us?' And within the hour they were on their way back to Jerusalem. There they found the eleven** (ἕνδεκα – *hendeka*) **disciples and the others who had gathered with them, who said, 'The Lord has really risen! HE APPEARED TO PETER!'"** *(See that?)*

The Emmaus disciples knew Jesus had already had a one-on-one meeting with Peter! How did they know that? Jesus had obviously told them in his long meeting with them! By the time they come to tell the other disciples, Peter had returned to be with them. The word "eleven" is there in the text and Judas is already dead. So, what finally gave Peter the guts to return and join with those he had so let down? Answer: Because he had already had a private meeting with Jesus, his risen Lord!

Sam, you are filling too many empty blanks with your own thoughts, No I'm not, and this is really important:

*"He appeared to Cephas* (Peter) *and then to the twelve." 1 Corinthians 15:5*

> Paul says: **1 Corinthians 15:4-5: "He was buried, and he was raised from the dead on the third day, just as the Scriptures said. He was seen by Peter (**Κηφᾶς – Cephas) **<u>and then</u> by the Twelve."** *(Actually 10 with Judas and Peter absent, but "The Twelve"-* δώδεκα, *became the general term for "Jesus' disciples.")*

So Jesus did, not only, instruct the angels to make sure they got word to Peter that he had risen, but Peter seems to be the first disciple Jesus seeks out. <u>The one who had so failed Jesus – Jesus seeks out first</u>! *(Do we see that?)*

1) Imagine that meeting! Did Jesus tell him that he was going to become a great leader of the Church? No!

2) How do we know that? Because we already know the conversation that is still to come by the Sea of Galilee a few days later that we've already initially looked at. Jesus asks Peter three times if he loves him and then tells Peter to "feed his lambs/sheep." *(Lead the flock – lead the Church!)*

3) That didn't happen in this first private meeting. So what did happen? We're not allowed, in Scripture, to look inside the room.

<u>But, you know what I imagine</u>? Peter had already received a message from the angels. He's sitting there mulling what he is going to say when he finally comes face to face with Jesus. Suddenly, there Jesus is in his newly risen, glorified body with nail prints in his hands and feet, standing inside Peter's front door.

Jesus had been at Peter's house in Capernaum many times. Tradition says that after Jesus left Nazareth, *(after his town's people in Nazareth had tried to throw him off a cliff),* he settled in Capernaum in a guest room on Peter's property. But that was all before Peter, *(after living some 800+ days of his recent life in close proximity with Jesus)* had so completely and publicly rejected his Lord.

Imagine Peter staring at the risen Jesus and then breaking down into uncontrollable sobs, just like when he ran out of the courtyard. It's not just sorrow for the denial it's all the never-ending arrogance and pride. It's all the trying to control Jesus with his loud, over-talking words. It's all the "becoming a mouthpiece for the devil" to the point Jesus had to tell him to "get behind me, satan."

All of that grief and sorrow had to come pouring out and I'm guessing Jesus' response was simply words of complete forgiveness with his arms wrapped around Peter hugging, and hugging, and hugging – with assurances that Peter's sin *(all of it)* was going to be separated from him as far as the east is from the west.

- If many of us relate to Peter in how sinful and falling-on-his-face he was, we also need to relate to what went on in that room that day – a complete sin-washing, a complete soul cleansing. Jesus was preparing the way for Peter to become totally restored, in fact to become the loudest voice again – but this time the loudest voice for truth and righteousness!

- I've often, in the last few years, invited people to "walk right into Jesus' outstretched arms of grace." I think I probably draw that word picture more for myself than the people to whom I am speaking. But the picture of Peter in that private room in Jerusalem that day, consumed with his own conviction of sin is such a good high-definition snapshot for each of us.
- Picture Peter walking into the outstretched arms of Jesus, and picture Jesus wrapping his arms around him speaking words of forgiveness and restoration!

Picture him doing the same thing for you! When the sins from your past haunt you, when satan *(the accuser)* uses those sins to try to convince you that you are useless and worthless to Jesus and the Kingdom of God – Picture Jesus wrapping his arms around you and saying, I'm cleansing you completely! I am washing your soul! And I promise you, as I "build my Church," I will most often use the very ones that others want to throw out! I will often build the "least likely" into the "most influential"!

*I do not call the qualified,*
*I qualify those I have called!*

So we let another week in Peter's life pass and find our way back to the side of the Sea of Galilee. We jumped in the last chapter to the fireside chat Jesus had with Peter beside the lake, asking him "Do you love me." *(x3)* We looked at the Greek words. We looked at Peter's response. I now want to watch the progression in Peter's mind and heart leading up to that "fireside chat."

Jesus meets #1) privately with Peter, #2) then all the disciples plus Peter, #3) then finally eight days later all the disciples including Peter, plus doubting Thomas who puts his fingers into Jesus' wounds. I carefully re-read the end of all four Gospels and the beginning of Acts. I was trying to really understand what all happened in the next 40 days before Jesus ascended back to Heaven.

**Acts 1:3 says: "During the forty days after he suffered and died, he appeared to the Apostles <u>from time to time</u>, and <u>he proved to them in many ways that he was actually alive</u>. And he talked to them about the Kingdom of God."** *(Imagine all the questions they would have had, and all the explanations Jesus would have given them.)*

Peter wouldn't have had any doubts after Jesus showed up in his room, with arms of forgiveness held wide. But what we surprisingly don't see – is Peter grabbing hold of Jesus' arm and not letting go for the next six weeks. We oddly don't find Jesus sitting on a street corner with lines of people waiting to ask him questions about his death and victorious resurrection. We only get the briefest glimpses into the words he told his disciples during those 40 days. *(Some are huge – like the expected arrival of the infilling Holy Spirit.)*

But, let's go back to the 1 Corinthians 15 passage. It has a few more clues. **1 Corinthians 15:4-9: "He**

**(Jesus) was buried, and he was raised from the dead on the third day, just as the Scriptures said. He was seen by Peter and then by the Twelve. After that, he was seen by more than 500 of his followers at one time, most of whom are still alive, though some have died. Then he was seen by James and later by all the apostles. Last of all, as though I had been born at the wrong time, I *(Paul)* also saw him. For I am the least of all the apostles."**

At some point, there was a large crowd gathered with Jesus. Those are people who would be dispersed, by persecution all over the Empire, but they would be loudly proclaiming for the next 50-60 years, Jesus died, but he rose from the dead! The Roman government and the Jewish leaders can spin their disinformation, but I was there. I saw him! I heard him with my own ears. I went up to him and touched the nail prints in his hands! He is without question, alive!

But the longest meeting recorded between the risen Jesus and his disciples that we get to look into is this meeting beside the Sea of Galilee. We skipped over a large chunk of the story in the last chapter to get to the campfire talk, so let's hit rewind for the next few minutes.

**John 21:1-3: "Later, Jesus appeared again to the disciples beside the Sea of Galilee. This is how it happened. Several of the disciples were there—Simon Peter, Thomas... Nathanael from Cana in Galilee, the sons of Zebedee, and two other**

**disciples. Simon Peter said, 'I'm going fishing.' 'We'll come, too,' they all said. So they went out in the boat, but they caught nothing all night."**

Like we exclaimed in the last chapter: "You're going to do what? You discovered 10-12 days ago that your crucified Lord has risen from the dead. He's out there somewhere and you're going where? You've got a whole world waiting to hear this resurrection message and you're going out to catch fish?" Maybe it wasn't their fault. Maybe they tried to find him and couldn't. Maybe Jesus had shut off his phone!

This all-night event ten days after the resurrection wasn't just seven guys going out for a relaxing evening of sport-fishing to clear their heads. This was seven guys going back to the commercial fishing trade that Jesus had called them away from three years earlier!

And notice the positioning of the names – it's not accidental! **John 21:2: Several of the disciples were there—Simon Peter and Thomas,** the Chief Denier and the Chief Doubter suddenly become post-resurrection fishing buddies! We know that this whole event was part of Jesus' plan to recall and commission these disciples *(not just Peter – all of them),* but it's hard for me to get my head around why they ended up back on that boat again!

## *GONE FISHING!*

The "gone fishing" sign wasn't just a sign on the door of their fishing office. It was a sign on the door of their hearts! Even though Jesus had now provably risen from the dead; even though Peter had one private meeting and two group meetings with Jesus even though Jesus had used their time together to teach them all amazing post-resurrection truths it still wasn't enough to completely turn the disciple's hearts in Jesus' direction, and only in Jesus' direction!

- "But, but, but; you guys are called, commissioned, 'disciples of the King of the Universe' who has just finished demonstrating his cosmic power by defeating death and rising from the dead!"
- "You are poised to be part of the biggest thing in the whole world, and you're out on a lake, fishing, and you're not even doing that well! You've fished all night and caught nothing!" Perhaps the "catching nothing" was an outer symbol of how these guys were still reacting on the inside? Maybe it was PTSD, a post-traumatic depression or something. But these guys are definitely not reacting *(in my opinion)* in the way logical thought would seem to dictate.

Is it possible for seven disciples to have a newly-risen, death-defeating Commander-in-Chief of the Universe, and still be depressed about where their lives are headed? Today, we all have a risen, death-defeating Commander-in-Chief of the Universe along with his outpoured, infilling, Holy Spirit. The Holy Spirit is transforming us from the inside out, and filling and empowering our daily lives, and leading us into all truth, and yet we are sometimes *(amazingly)* still depressed about where our lives are headed, aren't we?

CHAPTER 3

We read earlier, that some of us have had the "rooster crowing" in our lives maybe even this past week. Remember Jesus doesn't respond to that with anger. He comes looking for us with forgiveness and restoration. *(if we are willing).* And most of us have been through "gone-fishing" times, haven't we? Me too! *(I'll be back, Jesus, I'll let you know when!)* Some of us have "gone fishing" signs hammered into the "door of our lives" right now. Don't we?

Remember, this isn't about Jesus beating them *(or us)* down. That's the last thing in the world he is interested in. It's just that Peter, Thomas, Nathaniel, James and John had too much to compute. Their systems were overloaded! So they returned to what was comfortable, familiar, and predictable. They knew the peace of a quiet morning, the predictability of the rising sun, the net rubbing comfortably over old calluses, the waves slapping the hull.

- Ministry with Jesus had been exciting with constant new lessons, new truth, huge crowds, thousands being healed, some even being raised from the dead – there was a constant euphoria about their future!
- But then came Jesus' real victory, him being crucified in the sight of thousands, his life blood pouring out on the ground for the sins of all humanity, And then he provably, triumphantly rose from the dead!

Oddly now, even though they had seen him risen, spoken with him, touched him, listened to amazing teachings – at that exact moment he was not with them, their forward path was uncertain, they felt vulnerable, unsure of their future.

But their return to the familiar fishing spots doesn't help. They seemed to have lost their knack for fishing. A whole night went by, and they didn't catch even one little fish! All night long they had cast out their net, each time expecting a response. As the night progressed they became stiff, and cold, and felt more and more empty, both in their nets, and in their hearts!

*Let me try to apply this to us:* If God has called me to himself, and commissioned me to a life purpose larger than my job or vocation. And I'm sitting in a "cold boat" casting my net out over and over, and every day my net comes up empty and my heart even emptier – I may need to learn some "Peter lessons." Yes?

> **John 21:4-5: "At dawn, Jesus was standing on the beach, but the disciples couldn't see who he was. He called out, 'Fellows, have you caught any fish?' 'No,' they replied."** Peter undoubtedly thought, "Go away, nosey man" Peter perhaps even shouted - "Go away! It's bad enough to have fished all night and come up empty without some landlubber asking stupid questions." **John 21:6: "Then he** ***(Jesus)*** **said, 'Throw out your net on the right-hand side of the boat, and you'll get some!'"**

Peter was startled, a memory leaped into his mind. There was something about that commanding voice coming from a fog-shrouded figure on the shore." Let's try it, guys" – "you've got to be kidding, Peter." But they did, and they couldn't haul in the net because there were so many fish!

A familiar bell was ringing inside Peter's head. *(a two-year-old memory, recorded back in Luke 5)* **Luke 5:4-8: "When he had finished speaking, he said to <u>Simon</u>, 'Now go out where it is deeper, and let down your nets to catch some fish.' 'Master,' <u>Simon</u> replied, 'we worked hard all last night and didn't catch a thing. But if you say so, I'll let the nets down again.' And this time their nets were so full of fish they began to tear! When Simon Peter realized what had happened, he fell to his knees before Jesus and said, '<u>Oh, Lord, please leave me—I'm too much of a sinner to be around you</u>.'"**

Peter had learned so much since those early days and yet somehow he had learned so little. With the whole crucifixion, denial, resurrection, forgiveness thing behind him, <u>he is still acting in his own power doing his own self-directed thing</u>.

*Self-directed living will always lead to emptiness of soul!*

Jesus wanted them to know the blessing of living in complete no-holds-barred obedience! **John 21:7-8: "Then the disciple Jesus loved** *(John)* **said to Peter,**

**'It's the Lord!' When Simon Peter heard that it was the Lord, he put on his tunic *(for he had stripped for work)*, jumped into the water, and headed to shore. The others stayed with the boat and pulled the loaded net to the shore, for they were only about a hundred yards from shore."**

Peter fixed his eyes 300 feet through the morning fog, then without taking his eyes off his Lord; he swam, with all his strength, straight toward him! We tend to see just the Bible story version of this. 300 feet is a lot of strokes. Something is happening in Peter's mind and heart with every stroke.

- This is such a turning point in Peter's life. He's going to get to the shore and sit across the fire from Jesus, and hear the words: "Do you love me Peter, do you really love me?"
- We are, at this moment in time in our study, only a little over five weeks away from the day of Pentecost when the Holy Spirit will be poured out. Peter will get up to speak, and from his formerly uncontrollable mouth will come the words:

**Acts 2:22-24, 36-38: "God publicly endorsed Jesus the Nazarene by doing powerful miracles, wonders, and signs through him, as you well know. But God knew what would happen, and his prearranged plan was carried out when Jesus was betrayed. With the help of lawless Gentiles, you nailed him to a cross and killed him. But, God released him from the horrors**

**of death and raised him back to life, for death could not keep him in its grip! So let everyone in Israel know for certain that God has made this Jesus, whom you crucified, to be both Lord and Messiah!"**

**"Peter's words pierced their hearts, and they said to him and to the other apostles, 'Brothers, what should we do?' Peter replied, 'Each of you must repent of your sins and turn to God, and be baptized in the name of Jesus Christ for the forgiveness of your sins. Then you will receive the gift of the Holy Spirit.'"** That's Peter – about 38 days after his 100-yard swim!

1) Remember; Whatever stage you are at in this life, God doesn't call the qualified, he qualifies the called!

2) God's not looking for you to "shape up," he's looking for you to become willing for him to shape you up!

3) If you think you are miles and miles away from God ever being able to use your life – so was Peter, and look how God used him!

4) But we do need to become willing for God to reshape us into the person he planned for us to be when he put us on this planet!

*Prayer:* Oh God, I struggle with allowing you to change me! I'm so much like Peter in hanging onto my old sinful self and not allowing you to completely transform the old sinful me into a brand new righteous me. Dear God, I right now submit to your perfect plan for my life.

Make me willing for you to reshape me into the person you planned me to be when you put me on this planet!

# CHAPTER 3

# Chapter 4

*Peter's radical transformation in preaching and leadership.*

---

*Is this sounding too familiar*? Peter was the arrogant, big mouth, messed up, botched-up, bungler who Jesus chose to be his first disciple. He's listed first in all four disciple lists in the Gospels and then in a fifth list in Paul's Epistles, but then oddly he's not listed first anymore. What happened? We're going to find out in this chapter.

Jesus was calling the former arrogant big mouth to become a leader in his new Church. Peter's big untamed mouth is the same mouth Jesus would eventually choose to become a disciplined, righteous mouth. We said that there are more recorded spoken words of Peter than any other person in the New Testament. He *(apparently)* never stopped talking! But in his vacillating, impulsive, personality Jesus saw the makings of a leader!

Many of us, by now, have probably acknowledged that we see ourselves reflected in early Peter, *(Me too!)* But we say it like it is always a terrible thing. Jesus saw something in early Peter that we preachers tend not to put in our sermons.

*Here's a brand new fact:* Peter asked Jesus more questions than all the other disciples combined! Every word Peter said or wrote in the Bible, number less than 9,500. The average reader can read them all in 38 minutes. The truth is Peter probably said that many words every 38 minutes for the entire three years of Jesus' public ministry! Can't you hear Jesus saying, "Yes Peter, let me finish with this person and then I'll answer your next twelve piled up questions." Oddly *(or maybe not so oddly)* Jesus saw in that, the makings of a leader!

- I've had some parents say to me, "my child wears me down." Take heart, Peter's mom probably often sat crying in the corner of her room!
- My older sister was named Melody Faith, my next oldest sister was named Merrilee Hope, and with biblical planning I was intended to be a girl with the middle name of Love and instead out came a very active boy, the "never-stop-talking" Sammy arriving just 13 months after my sister.
- My mother eventually had *(what they called in those days)* a nervous breakdown. I've tried to blame that on my sister, although she was quiet and meek, two things I was not! There's a point here somewhere…
  1) When the soldiers come to arrest Jesus, and Peter whisks out his sword and tries to slice off Malchus' head, but only lops off an ear – Jesus heals the ear and scolds Peter. We talk about that like it was an

all-bad thing – but I wonder if Jesus saw in that impulsive personality someone who would be willing to stand up *(just 50 days after his resurrection)* in front of thousands of people and declare "You killed the Author of Life, but he didn't stay dead, God raised him from the dead!" Notice, none of the other disciples pulled their swords to defend Jesus and none of the others are listed as preaching on the day of Pentecost!

2) Remember when Peter got out of the boat in a storm to walk on the water toward Jesus. He lost faith when he saw the crashing sea, and sank. We preach messages about how Peter needed to have more faith – but don't forget, the other eleven disciples were all still huddled back in the boat! Peter was the only one with the impulsiveness and the guts, and the faith, to get out and try to walk on the water! That was the raw material that God chose to raise up a new church!

We see pictures of massive baptisms going on right now in the Philippines, Rwanda, Brazil, Iraq, and IRAN! We rejoice that God is moving mightily in this world.

The point is: somebody had to start all that! Somebody had to have the guts to stand up just days after the proclaimed Messiah had been publicly murdered, and say, "You all killed him, but he rose from the dead and he is now alive!" And who had more guts than the guy who lopped off Malchus' ear in front of a squadron of soldiers.

Yes. Peter "face-splatted" by denying Jesus! But Jesus didn't just reclaim Peter back into fellowship with him. Within ten days after his public denial of Jesus – Jesus is recalling Peter into ministry *(Feed my Sheep).* In fact, he's calling him to be the primary leader of the new just-ready-to-form "Christian" Church. After the arrival of the promised Holy Spirit, filling Peter and the other disciples with "Power from on High," it's not young John who climbs up to preach. It's not John's older brother Andrew, who was probably one of the oldest and most mature of the disciples. It is, in fact Peter – impetuous, fearless Peter the sword-carrying fisherman from Galilee, who climbs to a high place and starts to "preach." Peter wasn't trained to preach, he had very little formal religious education! How do we know that?

> **Acts 4:13: "The members of the council were amazed when they saw the boldness of Peter and John, for they could see that they were ordinary men with no special training in the Scriptures."**

That unlearned small-business owner, Peter, climbs up to a high visible place and with no preaching experience at all, cuts loose! He doesn't open up his notebook with computer generated notes. He has no notes! His first sermon is 653 words in English! About twelve minutes! *(Peter, the untrained fisherman!)* There are four quotes out of the Old Testament *(by memory),* a very long quote from Joel 2, and three different Psalms.

**Acts 2:22-23: "People of Israel, listen! God publicly endorsed Jesus the Nazarene by doing powerful miracles, wonders, and signs through him, as you well know. But God knew what would happen, and his prearranged plan was carried out when Jesus was betrayed. With the help of lawless Gentiles, you nailed him to a cross and you killed him!"**

Notice Peter is not saying this up in his hometown of Caesarea. He, "the knuckle-dragging Galilean" is shouting it out in Jerusalem. His audience includes the same Jews who just screamed for Jesus' death – and the same Roman soldiers who had nailed Jesus to a cross!

**Acts 2:24,36: "But God released him from the horrors of death** *(that you all inflicted on him)* **and raised him back to life, for death could not keep him in its grip… So let everyone in Israel know for certain that God has made this Jesus, whom you crucified, to be both Lord and Messiah!"** *(It had only been 6 months earlier up at Caesarea Philippi that he had first screamed at Jesus, "You are the Christ (the Messiah) the Son of the living God"!)* Now just 26 weeks later, here he is unfolding God's plan like a seasoned evangelist.

**Acts 2:37-38: "Peter's words pierced their hearts, and they said to him and to the other apostles, 'Brothers, what should we do?'** *(I don't know this, but I suspect the others were looking at each other saying, I don't know, what* *should they do?)* **Peter** *(of course)* **replied, '<u>Each of you must repent</u>** (μετανοέω) **<u>of your sins and turn to God</u>, and <u>be baptized</u> in the name of Jesus Christ for the forgiveness of your sins.'"**

- Many will say, the word "repent" in the Bible means "to change one's mind." And that is true; the New Testament Greek word "metanoia" is a compound word meaning exactly that. But I pulled every use of the word repent in both the Old and New Testaments and the whole meaning is much deeper than that.
- It doesn't mean "to change one's mind" like from mostly enjoying chocolate ice cream to liking vanilla. It means a total and complete change of one's mind and heart from darkness to light. A soul transforming turn around!

That's what the Hebrew word for repentance, *(TESHUVAH-repent, turn 180 degrees)*, means. That's the vividly clear example laid out in the Old Testament, including David's famous prayer of repentance in Psalm 51.

That's why I often use the phrase – "Repentance is a U-turn. You are going in one direction you make a u-turn and go in the exact opposite direction! It's not a partial change of one's mind – it is a complete transformation of one's direction." *Please see the five-part Bible study on*

*Repentance in Part Two of my last book:* ***Jonah – God's Unrelenting Grace.***

I was at a big outreach event, and the national speaker gave a wonderful call to come to Jesus and then offered the prayer of salvation. I was waiting for him to include the idea of repentance and he never did. I'm not bashing him, he's a wonderful God-anointed speaker, but I think many have lost sight of an important Biblical theology. It was taught the most by Jesus himself, and then secondly, by Peter!

Why was repentance such a big deal to Peter? Why was that what instantly popped into his mind when the listeners asked him, "Brothers, what do we do." Why did it explode out of his mouth to stress to them how much they needed a whole new mindset, a 180-degree U-turn? Because that is exactly what had happened to him!

Remember 53 days earlier he had been denying that he even knew Jesus! Four or five days after that, Jesus meets him in a private place and my mental picture of what happened in that private place is all wrapped up in this word repentance. Peter radically repented and Jesus overwhelmingly forgave!

That all figures into the conversation on the seaside a week later where Jesus is asking Peter, "Do you love me? Peter, you rejected me completely and I forgave and restored you completely. I do love you, Peter, with every fiber of my being and what I most want from you

– is for you to love me back with all your heart, mind, soul, and strength."

One chapter *(in Acts)* after his first sermon on the Day of Pentecost, a few days later in actual time – once again "fisherman Peter" is waxing eloquent in another sermon, and once again he is not mincing any words:

> **Acts 3:14-15, 17-18: "You rejected this holy, righteous one and instead demanded the release of a murderer. You killed the Author of Life, but God raised him from the dead. And we are witnesses of this fact! 'Friends, I realize that what you and your leaders did to Jesus was done in ignorance. But God was fulfilling what all the prophets had foretold about the Messiah—that he must suffer these things."**

> **Acts 3:19-21: "Now repent** (Μετανοήσατε) **of your sins and turn** (ἐπιστρέψατε) **to God, so that your sins may be wiped away.** (ἐξαλειφθῆναι) **Then times of refreshment will come from the presence of the Lord, and he will again send you Jesus, your appointed Messiah. For he must remain in heaven until the time for the final restoration of all things, as God promised long ago through his holy prophets."**

Μετανοήσατε – a complete change of mind *(from bound in sin to free in Christ).*

ἐπιστρέψατε – turn, turn around, to make a u-turn.

ἐξαλειφθῆναι – wholly wiped out, completely erased, obliterated.

- One interesting point here is that Peter is probably in his mid to late 30's at this time.
- By the time he writes I Peter, *(in his late-60's perhaps),* the unlearned fisherman is using some very learned Greek grammar.
- When we say God totally transformed Peter, we are saying quite a mouthful.

Let's move on in Peter's life story to Acts 4. By now the Jewish people have gotten over the initial shock of Jesus being crucified, the cosmos erupting in an eclipse of the sun, and a massive earthquake. The Jews had largely followed their religious leaders "spin" and rejected all accounts of Jesus' resurrection. They had started to form into an <u>organized opposition</u> to snuff out this rapidly forming "Christian" Church. Peter and young John are preaching in the temple.

> **Acts 4:1-4: "... they were confronted by the priests, the captain of the Temple guard, and some of the Sadducees. These leaders were very disturbed that <u>Peter and John were teaching the people that through Jesus there is a resurrection of the dead</u>. <u>They arrested them</u> and, since it was already evening, put them in jail until morning. But many of the people who heard their message believed it, so the <u>number of men who believed now totaled about 5,000</u>"** *(plus women and children).*

The next morning, after a hard night on the rock floor, they are brought into court, and for Peter the courtroom becomes a pulpit to preach another message. Soul-transformed, Spirit-filled Peter is getting spiritually bolder. He knows these people are capable of snuffing out his life, but he's not running like a scared rabbit the way he did when Jesus was hauled off to trial. He now seems to be thoroughly enjoying himself!

> **Acts 4:8-10, 12: "Then Peter, filled with the Holy Spirit, said to them, 'Rulers and elders of our people, are we being questioned today because we've done a good deed for a crippled man? Do you want to know how he was healed? Let me clearly state to all of you and to all the people of Israel that he was healed by the powerful name of Jesus Christ the Nazarene, the man you crucified but whom God raised from the dead... There is salvation in no one else! God has given no other name under heaven by which we must be saved.'"**

"Do you all understand? There is no other pathway to get to Heaven. We are not teaching anything other than what the ancient prophets already taught. They were so clear that a Messiah was coming. Humanity had broken apart their relationship with God. There was no human pathway to 'turn around.' Animal sacrifices were just put in place to cover the sins of people. Somebody had to come to earth who was sinless *(only God himself fits that picture),* who could take on himself the sins of humanity and pay their penalty. That is exactly what Isaiah 53 said was going to happen!" *And Daniel had defined it even further:*

**Daniel 9:25-26: "Now listen and understand! Seven sets of seven plus sixty-two sets of seven will pass** *(483 years)* **from the time the command is given to rebuild Jerusalem until a ruler—the Anointed One—comes. Jerusalem will be rebuilt with streets and strong defenses, despite the perilous times. After this period of sixty-two sets of seven, the Anointed One will be killed, appearing to have accomplished nothing."** "Check your calendars guys – it had been 483 since King Artexerxes decreed Jerusalem's walls to be rebuilt. The Anointed One came into Jerusalem riding on a donkey *(483 years later)* – but he was then killed, and you guys are his killers"!

Do we see why Jesus chose this "tough guy" to lead the Early Church? Some of Peter's greatest weaknesses, by God's grace, had become his greatest strengths! Shouldn't that ring all kinds of bells in our own lives?

**Acts 4:13: "The members of the council were amazed when they saw the boldness of Peter and John, for they could see that they were ordinary men with no special training in the Scriptures. They also recognized them as men who had been with Jesus."** Clearly that doesn't just mean they had walked the roads alongside of Jesus, **they had "been with Jesus"!**

- The members of the most elite council, in Jerusalem, were amazed! Peter and young John were probably more than a little amazed themselves! Nobody was more soul-deep amazed than ole deny-his-Lord Peter.

- Instead of pulling in nets of fish, he really had become "a fisher-of-men" just like Jesus had promised! But who would have thought that would have meant matching wits with some of the smartest, most educated, most powerful people in society, and amazingly – winning the arguments! Watch the confusion here; The smartest guys in Jerusalem become blubbering idiots:

**Acts 4:16-18: "'What should we do with these men?' they asked each other. 'We can't deny that they have performed a miraculous sign, and everybody in Jerusalem knows about it. But to keep them from spreading their propaganda any further, we must warn them not to speak to anyone in Jesus' name again.' So they called the apostles back in and commanded them never again to speak or teach in the name of Jesus."**

Yeah, that's going to work! Did they think Peter and John would say, "Ok, we'll shut up now! We believe we are teaching the biggest, most important truth that has ever touched humanity and will affect every human that has ever been born, or will ever be born in the future – but if you find our message offensive, we'll just keep it to ourselves."

I put this picture of a modern protest against "Christian Fascism" here on purpose. Fascism is "autocratic human government dictatorial control" – and nobody in history has been more harmed over the centuries by fascism than Christians *(Secondly the Jews).* And that is exactly what is going on right here with Peter and John, and their treatment by the Jewish religious leadership!

> **Acts 4:19-20: "But Peter and John replied, 'Do you think God wants us to obey you rather than him? We cannot stop telling about everything we have seen and heard.'"**

It's interesting to me that the two men being told that day to "shut their mouths" are responsible for seven books in your New Testament! Some of the most potent passages in all of inspired Scripture came from their pens. The lion's share of prophetic truths about the Second Coming of Jesus, and prophetic things yet to come here on this planet, come from the pens of the men who were told that day, "Don't you speak or teach about Jesus anymore"!

> By the time we get to **Acts 5:14-16: "Yet more and more people believed and were brought to the Lord—crowds of both men and women. As a result of the apostles' work, sick people were brought out into the streets on beds and mats so that Peter's shadow might fall across some of them as he went by. Crowds came from the villages around Jerusalem, bringing their sick and those possessed by evil spirits, and they were all healed."**

- Man, this is heady stuff. The man who couldn't keep his foot out of his mouth, is suddenly at the top of the spiritual heap. Even his shadow brought healing!

- He's the guy who first gets a message from God and takes the Gospel to the Gentiles. He's the guy who then tries to convince his fellow Jewish Believers that Jesus died for the Gentiles too!

You would have thought the rest of the New Testament would/should be 3rd Peter, 4th Peter, 8th Peter, 12th Peter, and then 1,2,3 John, Jude, and Revelation! But that's not what happens, at all. A violent murderer of Christians, named Saul meets Jesus on the Road to Damascus; when he is finally ready to be used by God, he searches out, stays with, and talks to… *(you guessed it)* Peter!

And why would he not? Peter was the undisputed leader of Jesus' church for 15 years. But then something odd happens. Within a few sentences Peter almost disappears out of the pages of Scripture! The story of the life of Paul, the murderer turned Apostle to the Gentiles, takes over.

Did you know that Peter also went on missionary journeys? Where do you read about them? Where do we learn about the great victories Peter saw as he proclaimed his risen Savior? We don't! Did you know that unlike Paul, Peter had a wife, and that Peter and his wife travelled together on missionary journeys? That is in the Bible! *(Your homework before we get to the next chapter is to find out where.)*

Clement of Alexandria wrote that Mrs. Peter was martyred for her faith before Peter's own death. There is so much to tie together in our minds between Mr. and

Mrs. Peter's martyrdom, and the words he writes in 1 Peter. We'll look hard at that in the next chapter.

The sections of Scripture we do have about Peter, after the book of Acts, is somewhat startling, confusing, and disheartening – but when I tied it to what Peter wrote in 1 Peter, I saw a picture that I've never seen before.

> *Paul:* **Galatians 2:7-9: "Instead, they saw that God had given me** *(Paul)* **the responsibility of preaching the gospel to the Gentiles, just as he had given Peter the responsibility of preaching to the Jews. For the same God who worked through Peter as the apostle to the Jews also worked through me as the apostle to the Gentiles. In fact, James, Peter, and John, who were known as pillars of the church, recognized the gift God had given me, and they accepted Barnabas and me as their co-workers. They encouraged us to keep preaching to the Gentiles, while they continued their work with the Jews."**

- Did you see what just happened there? For the first time, Peter's name is not at the top of the list. James' name is! Peter didn't retire, He was only in his mid- 50's.
- He, who used to walk around Jerusalem with his shadow healing people, has been replaced by Jesus' kid-brother, James, who didn't even believe in Jesus until after the resurrection!
- Then tough old former-murderer Apostle Paul adds this:

## *I had to oppose him to his face – I told Peter in front of everyone!*

**Galatians 2:11-14: "But when Peter came to Antioch, I had to oppose him to his face, for what he did was very wrong. When he first arrived, he ate with the Gentile believers, who were not circumcised. But afterward, when some friends of James came, Peter wouldn't eat with the Gentiles anymore. He was afraid of criticism from these people who insisted on the necessity of circumcision. As a result, other Jewish believers followed Peter's hypocrisy, and even Barnabas was led astray by their hypocrisy. When I saw that they were not following the truth of the gospel message, I said to Peter in front of all the others, 'Since you, a Jew by birth, have discarded the Jewish laws and are living like a Gentile, why are you now trying to make these Gentiles follow the Jewish traditions?'"**

- Seasoned Peter is being publicly shamed by a new upstart that he brought into ministry!
- The old Peter would have verbally torn Paul limb from limb. He would have reminded Paul that "he had spent some 800 days of his life in the direct presence of Jesus – he didn't meet him in a vision on a dusty road."
- He might have reminded Paul that he was already leading the church while Paul was still running around killing Christians.

- He could have mentioned that he had faced off with the highest level Pharisees of which Paul had been a low level one – and he, Peter, had beaten them!

He didn't do any of that! We see a very different man than we met before Pentecost. For the first time, we're starting to be able to link Peter's "new attitude" to what eventually shows up in the words of his first Epistle:

> **1 Peter 2:21-24: "For God called me to do good even if it means suffering, just as Christ suffered for me. He is my example, and I must follow in his steps. He never sinned, nor ever deceived anyone. He did not retaliate when he was insulted, nor threaten revenge when he suffered. He left his case in the hands of God, who always judges fairly. He personally carried my sins in his body on the cross so that I can be dead to sin and live for what is right. By his wounds I am healed!"**

# Chapter 5

*Peter takes the Gospel to the World!*

---

We are at a part of Peter's life that isn't often included in sermons, but we need to see this. Remember we've been looking for a sinful person who turned righteous and was mightily used by God! Peter does, Peter is! Now Peter has been forgiven and commissioned to lead Jesus' newly forming Church. On the day of Pentecost, first 3,000 believed and then 20,000 – and then the number explodes to many, many thousands.

Let me show you a passage in Acts, parts of which we might sometimes overlook. *(It's the "stoning of Stephen" passage.)*

> **Acts 8:1-4: "Saul was one of the witnesses and he agreed completely with the killing of Stephen. A great wave of persecution began that day, sweeping over the church in Jerusalem; and all the Believers except the Apostles were scattered through the**

**regions of Judea and Samaria... But Saul was going everywhere to destroy the church. He went from house to house, dragging out both men and women to throw them into prison. But the Believers who were scattered preached the Good News about Jesus wherever they went."** Two of those verses talk about the despicable murderer Saul who becomes the Apostle to the Gentiles, Paul. The other two talk about the persecution of the Church!

We studied in the last chapter, how Peter for the first 15 years after Jesus' ascension became the undisputed head of the Jerusalem Church. He was a spiritual powerhouse! People would bring their sick hoping that Peter's shadow would fall on them and they would be healed. Up through Acts 12, Peter is front and center – and then starting in Acts 13, Peter almost disappears from the historical accounting of Scripture, and Paul jumps onto the front stage for the rest of the book of Acts and for 13 of the Epistles. We saw in the Acts 8:1-4 passage on the preceding page that two of the verses introduce the Christian-murdering Saul – but the other two verses we tend to treat as filler – and they're not!

**Acts 8:2-4, 4: "A great wave of persecution began that day, sweeping over the church in Jerusalem; and all the Believers except the Apostles were scattered through the regions of Judea and Samaria. But the Believers who were scattered preached the Good News about Jesus wherever they went."**

> When Paul says, in Galatians 4, that Jesus was born in the fullness of time what did he mean? The Romans *(terrible pagans that they were)* had forced every part of the Empire to learn and use the Greek language, that's why God inspired the New Testament to be written in Greek! No matter what one's ethnicity, they could read the newly forming Bible.
> It was the first time in history a single language could reach the whole world. Secondly, the Romans were good builders, and they built an amazing road system into every part of the Empire, connecting every conquered country into one single travelable unit.

So, the Acts 2 "great wave of persecution sweeping over the Church" drove all the Believers in Jerusalem *(except the Apostles)* out into the provinces of Israel, but as they were scattered, "they preached the Good News about Jesus wherever they went."

- It must have been so tough on early Christian families because the persecution eventually got so fierce that parents, trying to protect their Jesus-following families, were pushed completely out of Israel altogether into surrounding pagan countries.
- Then persecution in the whole Roman Empire took root, and that pushed Christians further and further outward across the Empire – traveling on those nice, stone Roman roads, spreading the Gospel of a crucified and risen Jesus to more and more pagan countries using the government-mandated Greek language. "In the fullness of time" Jesus came!

Observation #1: God's eternal plan for our lives doesn't always guarantee smooth sailing, but if we will allow Jesus to shape us and use us, regardless of our circumstances, He will achieve "maximum eternal impact" in and through our lives!

One of the people whose eternal ministry moves him out of Jerusalem – was Peter! Remember, we saw in the last chapter that James, Jesus' kid brother, becomes the head of the Jerusalem church. Peter moves toward Samaritan territory leading them to faith in Jesus and then crosses over into foreign countries leading pure pagan Gentiles into the faith.

Have we all noticed the significance of this passage:

**Acts 9:32-42: "Meanwhile, Peter traveled from place to place, and he came down to visit the believers in the town of Lydda. There he met a man named Aeneas, who had been paralyzed and bedridden for eight years. Peter said to him, "Aeneas, Jesus Christ heals you! Get up, and roll up your sleeping mat!" And he was healed instantly. Then the whole population of Lydda and Sharon saw Aeneas walking around, and they turned to the Lord.**

**"There was a believer in Joppa** *(The same seaport town where Jonah had boarded a ship to run away from God)* **named Tabitha. She was always doing kind things for others and helping the poor. About this time she became ill and died. Her body was washed for burial and laid in an upstairs room. But the Believers had heard that Peter was nearby at Lydda, so they sent**

**two men to beg him, 'Please come as soon as possible!' So Peter returned with them; and as soon as he arrived, they took him to the upstairs room.**

**"The room was filled with widows who were weeping and showing him the coats and other clothes Tabitha had made for them. But Peter asked them all to leave the room; then he knelt and prayed. Turning to the body he said, 'Get up, Tabitha.' And she opened her eyes! When she saw Peter, she sat up! He gave her his hand and helped her up. Then he called in the widows and all the Believers, and he presented her to them alive. The news spread through the whole town, and many believed in the Lord."**

*So, what was Peter thinking right about then?*

There was that time *(in Luke 22)* right after the Last Supper, *(after Judas slinks out of the room)* when the other disciples *(including Peter)* got into a heated argument about who was going to be the greatest in Jesus' kingdom. Was any of that arrogance left in Peter after the crucifixion, the resurrection, his restoration, the filling of the Holy Spirit and his sermons on and after the day of Pentecost?

After the Acts 9 miracles on the preceding page, is Peter "sending a text" to the other disciples saying, "Man, you ought to see what I just did. I just raised a dead woman back to life. Jesus raised just four dead people *(that are recorded in Scripture)*. I'm already 25% on the way to catching up with our Lord"! NO!

Remember, back in Jerusalem people had been bringing sick people just to catch a piece of Peter's shadow – but Peter left Jerusalem! We don't know exactly when James began to lead the church *(and Peter began traveling from place to place - Acts 9:32)*, but it must have already happened. We are not ever told why the switch in leadership took place, but I have a gut feeling that Peter may have thought something like "People are putting too much emphasis on me, and losing sight of the fact that I am just a servant of my risen Lord."

When Peter meets Cornelius the Roman officer, Cornelius "falls down and worships" Peter. *(Acts 10)* Peter is horrified, "Get up Sir, I'm just a fallen, human being"! Jesus, on the other hand, died by hanging on a cross, but God raised him to life on the third day! He's the one you should worship, even as a Gentile! That was a big day in Peter's life, in all of Christianity! Most of us reading this book are probably Gentiles, we need to thank Peter someday for his willingness to stop promoting himself and point the Gentiles to Jesus!

> Observation #2: God "achieving maximum eternal impact" in and through our lives, may not look anything like what we envision. God's divine plans often look very little like our self-focused human plans! God is God, and we are not!

When Peter does go back to Jerusalem in the 12th chapter of Acts, James *(the older brother of young teen-age John)*, has just had his head sliced off by evil King Herod Agrippa. It happened just before Passover. Acts 12 says the Jews were so pleased that one of the leaders of the "blasphemous Christian sect" had been publicly executed, that Herod Agrippa, filled with adrenalin, then grabbed *(former Jerusalem Church leader)* Peter who had come into town for the feast and slapped him in a prison cell undoubtedly planning to slice his head off too.

Herod Agrippa, Grandson of Herod the Great, was an evil dude. He was educated in Rome. He was "elbow deep" in the assassination of Emperor Caligula which opened the door for Mad Nero to take the throne. *(Emperor Nero was the one who would start the horrifying Roman wave of persecution against the Christians that would eventually end in the execution of Peter and Paul.)* Partly-Jewish Herod got a "little throne" in Israel as a reward for his treachery, and after the applause for killing a perfectly innocent James, he has Peter locked up in prison undoubtedly getting ready for a fake trial and quick execution after the feast.

> Observation #3: When it seems like the "Herod Agrippa's" of your life have you in their crosshairs whether it be people, or circumstances, or sickness, or your job, or financial concerns, look up! No one is more interested in your eternal well-being than God is! While other people may not have your best interest at heart, God always, always does! No one is more interested in your ultimate success than God is, and no

one is more prepared to make that into an eternal reality than your Creator!

Agrippa is at the zenith of power, he has Peter in his bull's-eye, and he's sharpening his sword for the morning after Passover. But remember God is God, and we are not!

**Acts 12:6-11: "The night before Peter was to be placed on trial, he was asleep, fastened with two chains between two soldiers. Others stood guard at the prison gate."** Herod might be evil but he wasn't stupid. He had enough Jewish biblical knowledge to know he was pitting himself against the God who had split the Red Sea!

**" Suddenly, there was a bright light in the cell, and an angel of the Lord stood before Peter. The angel struck him on the side to awaken him and said, 'Quick! Get up!' And the chains fell off his wrists. Then the angel told him, 'Get dressed and put on your sandals.' And he did. 'Now put on your coat and follow me,' the angel ordered.**

**"So Peter left the cell, following the angel. But all the time he thought it was a vision. He didn't realize it was actually happening. They passed the first and second guard posts and came to the iron-gate leading to the city, and this opened for them all by itself. So they passed through and started walking down the street, and then the angel suddenly left him. Peter finally came to his senses. 'It's really true!' he said. 'The Lord has sent his angel and saved me from**

**Herod and from what the Jewish leaders had planned to do to me!'"**

Principle #4: Whatever "impossible situations" are right now present in your life – your trust cannot rest in other people, or in the feeble human plans we ourselves have made. Our trust cannot be in doctors or pharmaceutical companies, governments, or political parties, or in people who promise us great wealth, or who promise us they can protect the wealth we already have. Our trust cannot be in those who guarantee us personal safety from harm. *(Although we appreciate some of the above enormously.)*

What Peter knew beyond all doubt *(In My Opinion)* was that hanging around Jerusalem *(for him at least)* was not the best pathway to building the kingdom of God! Jesus had said to him directly, "I will build my church and the gates of hell/hades will not prevail against it!" When Jesus said that, Peter probably first thought that meant just building Jesus' Church inside Israel, it didn't, not for him! Peter's reaction surely was that Jesus was talking only about his chosen people, the Jews. Nope, he wasn't!

The Church of Jesus was exploding in size. But the real growth explosion of the church was now taking place "out there" in ever-expanding circles outside Jerusalem and even outside Israel. So where does Peter decide to spend the rest of his life? "Out there, in ever-expanding circles around Jerusalem and outside Israel!" How do you know that Sam? Let me unfold some often-overlooked thoughts here for a few pages:

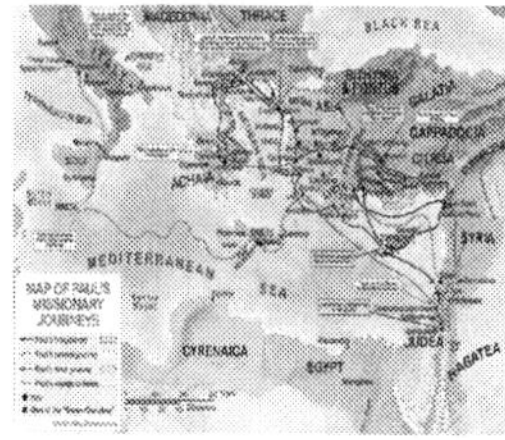

Tradition says that Peter travelled on missionary journeys just like Paul did! We know all about Paul's three missionary journeys because they are all spelled out in the book of Acts.

Peter's story disappears after Acts 12, so that Paul and Barnabus' journey can be described starting in Acts 13.

So what did happen to Peter after Acts 12? He surely didn't move to a beach house on the Mediterranean and call it quits. As we said, he's probably only in his mid 50's at that time and he will not die at the hand of Nero, until his late 60's. We are familiar with the people and places of Paul's missionary journeys.

But imagine the power of Peter's testimony! All of the things we have been talking about the last four chapters. "I was such an arrogant, self-assured, self-sovereign jerk-of-a-man. In spite of all my failings, Jesus called me to be his first disciple! I've already stated that everything Peter said or wrote can be read in 38 minutes – but he was with Jesus for three whole years! Imagine the first-hand stories Peter would have told in the churches he visited, stories that aren't included in the Bible! Imagine him personally standing up in front of new churches in Asia and telling the account of his betrayal, and describing the heart-wrenching sobs that came out of his mouth as he realized he had turned traitor on the man he himself called, the Messiah, the Son of the living God! Imagine him telling the story of the resurrection, first-hand, and how Jesus had come and visited him personally offering him forgiveness and freedom from his past.

As much as we have come to love the Apostle Paul – Paul didn't have many first-hand stories to tell. He had one meeting with Jesus *(in a vision)* on the road to Damascus. He had never spent one whole day of his life in the actual, personal presence of Jesus. Think of the impact Peter would have had as he travelled from church to church. Imagine the excitement as people gathered to hear "the great Peter" speak!

> Observation #5: God can/will take what we may think are the lowest seasons of our life, and turning them into eternal spiritual fruit-bearing seasons if we will just yield to his loving, guiding hand!

I said in the last chapter that, unlike Paul, Peter did have a wife. *(The truth is Paul probably started out with one too. He was a Pharisee, and Pharisees weren't allowed to be unmarried.)* But here is the proof about Peter from the pages of Scripture:

> **Matthew 8:14-15: "When Jesus arrived at Peter's house, Peter's mother-in-law was sick in bed with a high fever. But when Jesus touched her hand, the fever left her. Then she got up and prepared a meal for him."** Clearly, you can't have a mother-in-law unless you have a wife! "Well maybe Mrs. Peter died and he was a widower?" Nope!

**1 Corinthians 9:4-5: "Don't we have the right to live in your homes and share your meals? Don't we have the right to bring a believing wife with us as the other apostles and the Lord's brothers do, <u>and as Peter does</u>?"**

Paul writes that many of the Apostles had wives! Paul is writing this from his missionary journeys into Corinth and he is saying that Mr. Peter and Mrs. Peter were traveling together in mission work! Which was stunning in itself, at a time when women were considered inferior, and men, in that society, often traveled around not even remotely being faithful in their marriage. The Apostles, including Peter, were setting a brand new example!

*Here is the next shocker.* All of this was happening at a time when persecution by the Romans had started to whip into high gear. The Roman poly-theists *(many-gods)* had decided that among all the different kinds of idol worshippers that the Roman Empire had conquered and had absorbed into the Roman Empire – the Christians were the ones they were most determined to despise.

- As we have already described, the pagan Romans were famous for sacrificing other humans. It was widely practiced that sacrificing one's own child to an idol was perfectly legal and beneficial.
- The Romans could even kill their own unwanted child up until age 8 with no legal punishment whatsoever.

But if you were a Christian and said there was only one true God in the universe, and that God sent his only Son to pay the sin penalty for all humanity, that was a crime punishable by imprisonment or death! The Romans began to call those people "atheists." Imagine that! The Romans prided themselves on being "tolerant." They tolerated the most awful and obscene things. The only people that they collectively decided should not be "tolerated" were the Christ-followers. <u>Does this sound at all familiar to us in modern times</u>?

This quote comes from Darwin Bedford's website. He calls himself the Atheist Messiah. "It may appear that

this is a hate site, but in fact, this is a love site. If that self-made $%*&! returns, we should kill him again! If Earth is to remain an ever-lasting paradise, then socially we need to denormalize religion because it is so harmful. Religion is harmful at every level. Religion harms individuals, families, communities, countries, and the world as a whole. Religion harms individuals by masking the truth. When an individual believes that there is a life after death and that a God wants them to behave in a certain manner, they are no longer living a spiritually free life. Religion harms families by splitting them apart when members deviate from the family's faith. Religion harms communities when members of each faith collect in areas and then conflict with each other.

I'm not advocating that we kill a real living person. Jesus is as make-believe as Kenny in South Park. It's OK for South Park to kill Kenny in many episodes, so it should be OK to suggest that we kill the fictional character, Jesus, a second time. So killing Jesus again is not a hate crime, it is a joke with attitude." *This is not at all funny, because we see this "attitude" exploding across our society, don't we?* Christians are the bad people! Christians are the immoral ones! Not tolerating any and all other beliefs is the worst possible kind of immorality!

- That is exactly what was happening in the Roman Empire: Imagine people who absorbed any and all the god's of the pagan idols around them into their pantheistic religions, but would call those who believe in only one God, "**atheists.**"
- The Roman leadership said the Christians were "**superstitious**." They started calling them **"haters of humanity."** Imagine that, the most loving, caring, compassionate people in the Empire, who took the discarded babies into their own families, and started small orphanages for thrown-away children, and nursed the sick and dying that no one else cared anything about – they were "haters of humanity!"

Understand, this was the society that Peter and his wife were traveling around in, evangelizing in, seeing pagans and Jews converted in, establishing churches, and re-visiting existing churches. But by this time in history, a church might be missing a whole family from one week to the next, because the "tolerant" Roman society just made them disappear! They were "haters of humanity" because they didn't accept every Roman perversion!

At some point Peter begins to write the inspired thoughts that show up in his first Epistle. I've never connected what he was writing to what was going on around him in Roman society every day, but when we do, it is startling! *(Can you imagine the people who were first reading these words from Peter's pen?)*

**1 Peter 1:6-7: "So be truly glad. There is wonderful joy ahead, even though you must endure many trials for a little while. These trials will show that your faith is genuine. It is being tested as fire tests and purifies gold—though your faith is far more precious than mere gold. So when your faith remains strong through many trials, it will bring you much praise and glory and honor on the day when Jesus Christ is revealed to the whole world."**

**1 Peter 4:1-2: "So then, since Christ suffered physical pain, you must arm yourselves with the same attitude he had, and be ready to suffer, too. For if you have suffered physically for Christ, you have finished with sin. You won't spend the rest of your lives chasing your own desires, but you will be anxious to do the will of God."**

**1 Peter 4:12-13: "Dear friends, don't be surprised at the fiery trials you are going through, as if something strange were happening to you. Instead, be very glad—for these trials make you partners with Christ in his suffering, so that you will have the**

**wonderful joy of seeing his glory when it is revealed to all the world."**

Are you now getting inside the minds of the Early Church who are first receiving those words? The insults of "You're an atheist, you're "immoral!" have now become government goons showing up in the middle of the night to take them away for an "attitude adjustment." I'm not making this stuff up. Pliny the Elder, a prominent first century author, *(and naval commander),* openly wrote, that "if, when persecuted the Christians recanted, they should be forgiven and allowed back into society – but if they refused, they should be given the worst kind of punishment as a lesson to all the other "immoral atheists."

And then along came Emperor Mad Nero! His mother Agrippina convinced her weak husband Claudius to promote her adopted son ahead of his firstborn son. She then murdered her husband cementing her spineless son's rule at 17 years of age. *(Obviously, it was to be her rule!)* Emperor Nero, not long into his adult life, had that conniving mother stabbed to death for treason. He then has his wife beheaded and publicly displayed her head for his mistress, a mistress that he then personally kicked to death when she was pregnant. These are the people who openly called Christians immoral! And this is the exact period of time that Peter and Mrs. Peter are ministering across the Empire and eventually into Rome itself. Nero cuts loose with a massive wave of persecution!

Principle # 6 If you are mocked for your faith, if you are rejected for your faith, if you are persecuted for your faith in Jesus – never, never, never give up or give in! "**Don't be surprised at the fiery trials you are going through as though something strange were happening to you. Instead, be very glad—for these trials will make you partners with Jesus Christ in his suffering" 1 Peter 4:12-13**! Do we see it? The Early Church considered suffering a huge positive!

The Roman Catholic Church teaches that Peter became the first Bishop of the Church in Rome, and that he was the leader of that church for some 20 years. The problem is, there is absolutely nothing written in first century history to suggest that is true. Ignatius, in his "Letter to Rome," 70 years later, puts Peter there at the very end of his life as does Irenaeus writing 120 years later. He was obviously in Rome at some point in his journeys *(maybe more than once)*, and he almost certainly died there. But the evidence shows him travelling throughout Asia Minor until not long before his death. When did he die? How did he die? How did Mrs. Peter die? *(We're coming to that!)* One more observation for this chapter:

Observation # 7: If you have made it through the early lessons that we learned from Peter's life, and the arrogance and self-assurance has been *(are being)* transformed away – if your attraction to sin has been increasingly "sanctified," and any thoughts about slipping off the path have been fading into the background of your mind – Run straight ahead toward the ribbon. Don't turn to the right or the left. Don't stop! Always, always do the next right(eous) thing!

# Chapter 6

*Peter's Humiliation and Missionary Journeys.*

---

Here's a short quiz: Everyone who gets it right – will receive the satisfaction of a job well done!

#1) T or F: We have, in the last four chapters, watched Peter, through the power of his crucified and risen Lord, turn from a bumbling, stumbling, self-centered, arrogant, immature fisherman into a Spirit-filled, Spirit-led mighty man of God who God used to spiritually transform many, many Jewish and Gentile lives! *True!*

#2) T or F: Unschooled, unlearned, small-business-man Peter is the disciple we get to watch on the day of Pentecost *(and then in successive sermons)* telling crowds, "You killed the Messiah, but God raised him from the dead. If you will repent and believe, your sins can be blotted out!" *True!*

It is worth pointing out again, it wasn't Paul who opened up the Gospel to the Gentiles – it was Peter! Imagine him wrestling with all the racist thoughts instilled in his Jewish mind that the Gentiles were not worthy of God's saving grace. Remember, God gives Peter a vision of a sheet let down from Heaven full of unclean animals, and then a visit with the Roman officer Cornelius, and he realizes that the death of Jesus was not just for the Jews, but for every human who would ever be born!

We noticed, as the Church moved in ever widening circles away from Jerusalem, Peter moved with them. In Acts 9:32 we read "meanwhile, Peter traveled from place to place." We found him in the last chapter, healing people on the Samaritan border and raising a dead woman back to life in the seaport of Joppa. And then after Acts 12, Peter almost disappears from Scripture.

> #3) T or F: After Acts 12, Peter virtually disappears from the pages of Scripture because he traded in his fishing boat for one of those sleek new wind-driven sailing yachts, and he and Mrs. Peter took early retirement and sailed around the Mediterranean? *False!*

Can you imagine any kind of situation where God would spend so much time sorting out Peter's arrogance and immaturity, and then just abandon him and turn his attention to the new Apostle to the Gentiles, Paul? That's what the Bible seems to do. In chapter 13 we get caught up in Paul's life and writings and forget there even was a Peter. Until we read Peter's two letters near the end of the New Testament. And we say, "Oh yeah, that guy. Maybe he didn't turn in his fishing boat for a sailing yacht, after all."

Seriously, I went through Bible College and Seminary, and I don't remember anybody ever teaching me what happened to Peter after Acts 12. There are only two other events about Peter listed in the New Testament. In fact I looked up every use of Peter's name from Acts 12 on, and his name is used only 14 more times. Two more times in Acts, 10 times by Paul in his Epistles and two times by Peter himself, in the first lines of his Epistles.

The "ten mentions by Paul" are a bit deceptive because most of them represent just two days in Peter's later life and for just a few minutes out of those days, and they are not very positive. You would think that "newbie" Paul would be praising the man who, though he denied Jesus three times, became such a powerhouse that, when he spoke on and after the day of Pentecost people were falling in repentance in front of the crucified and risen Messiah.

You/I would think that Paul would be deferring to Peter saying "Nobody in all of the new Christian Church has been responsible for more people coming to faith in Jesus than stumbling, bumbling Peter, turned mighty warrior of the cross of Christ!" But that's not what we read in Scripture!

*Paul protested Peter to his face concerning his conduct!*

*Again, but even more:* **Galatians 2:11-14: "But when Peter came to Antioch, I had to oppose him to his face, for what he did was very wrong. When he first arrived, he ate with the Gentile believers, who were not circumcised. But afterward, when some friends of James came, Peter wouldn't eat with the Gentiles**

**anymore. He was afraid of criticism from these people who insisted on the necessity of circumcision. As a result, other Jewish believers followed Peter's hypocrisy, and even Barnabas was led astray by their hypocrisy. When I saw that they were not following the truth of the gospel message, I said to Peter in front of all the others, 'Since you, a Jew by birth, have discarded the Jewish laws and are living like a Gentile, why are you now trying to make these Gentiles follow the Jewish traditions?'"**

Principle #1: If you are a younger person reading this book, make sure you don't look at an older or more seasoned Christian person and miss the depth of knowledge and wisdom that now fills them. Cherish them, talk with them. Learn from them! People of great influence grow old and frail!

While, and just before, I was writing this material I had to say goodbye to some very dear people in our church. This passage made me think of them. Jerry Katzman used to fly planes onto aircraft carriers. Mike Richards used to fly jets around the world carrying European royalty. George Korzec used to face off with bad guys as a detective in the streets of Buffalo. Jim McGrath *(who's not dead but was listening when I first presented this material)* was an air traffic controller who stood face to face with Mohammad Atta in a control tower in Miami before Atta flew a plane into the World Trade Towers. Don't make the mistake, younger people, of looking at mature people across the aisle in your church and miss the fact that they have much to teach you!

I'm very aware that I am dealing with inspired Scripture in Galatians 2, but <u>who said Peter did what he did that day because he was afraid</u>? <u>Paul did</u>! If we had a chance to hear Peter's take on that day, it may have sounded very different.

- Who was the first guy who led a Gentile to the Lord and then invited him into his house and ate with him! Peter!
- Peter had to be thinking as Paul was rebuking him. "Dude, I was leading the new Christian Church, bringing thousands of people into Jesus' kingdom while you were running around like a rabid wolf grabbing people out of the Church, hauling them off to jail, and having them executed!
- "Who do you think you are, you upstart evangelist wanna-be, to be dressing me down in public? If you have a problem with me why aren't you pulling me into a quiet room, the way mature people do?"

### *Galatians: The Gospel of Grace!*

If you have studied the Bible much, you will understand that Paul's letter to the Galatians was all about living in grace vs. living under the law – so we can understand why Paul put this angry Galatians 2 outburst against Peter into that letter. But as I've studied it, about an equal number of scholars seem to think Peter was out of place vs. those who think Paul was showing immature disrespect.

I don't know if this ever really caught my attention before: In **Galatians 1:13: "Paul admits that he persecuted the church. 'I tried to destroy it,'"** he says. But once Jesus got hold of his heart, Paul headed south past Mt Sinai, further into the desert of what is now Saudi Arabia for three years. Just he and God, as God washed out much of the sinful crud in his mind and soul.

Principle #2: God is all about shaping our lives to have "maximum eternal impact." The most effective shaping times in our lives typically don't happen sitting beside a lake, sipping a glass of lemonade *(Once in a while God does speak to us deeply sitting beside a lake).* Often our greatest spiritual growth comes right in the middle of us grinding through difficult life circumstances. Watch this, when God was ready, Paul came back to Jerusalem.

*Galatians 1:18: "Three years later I went to Jerusalem to get to know Peter, and I stayed with him for fifteen days!"*

There are ancient conversations we would love to peer into. This is one of them. We can imagine two weeks of deep, intense, heart-to-heart discussions, where Peter fills in all the gaps in what we have been discussing for the last five chapters.

Peter probably would have said he understood murderous Saul as he raged his way across Israel killing Christians. He would have testified how his own deeply arrogant, sinful heart had been so radically transformed by the power of Jesus' death and resurrection, and then Jesus' infilling Holy Spirit!

I am convinced that some of what we see as deep theologies in Paul's Epistles spawned out of those two weeks of intense discipleship at Peter's house– as Paul soaked up Peter's words, scribbles notes furiously and asks thousands of questions. Peter would have *(In My Opinion)* shared with Paul hundreds of things that Jesus personally told him, that we do not have in our Bible. We can read all the words said by Jesus in the Bible in 4 hours. Peter and Paul talked for 15 days! All of the above makes the public conflict a few months later seem so odd to me!

> Principle #3: Don't imagine that being with people of like-Christian faith is going to cause you to see eye-to-eye perfectly. Don't forget, Paul would have another conflict with Barnabas that would split them into two teams. The conflict was about John Mark. Paul didn't trust him. But Mark went on to write a Gospel in your Bible. He turned out to be a good guy after all!

In fact, this slammed into my head as I was writing this material. Peter in his first Epistle writes, **1 Peter 5:13: "Your sister church here in Babylon** *(Rome)* **sends you greetings, and <u>so does my son Mark</u>!"** Tradition says this is the same Mark that Paul rejected *(John Mark)*. He's now with Peter in Rome in the last few months/years of Peter's life. Most say, he had become a "spiritual son" to Peter. What if that's not the case?

What if he is Peter's real son, now in Rome with his Dad? *(I've looked closely and that is not a textual impossibility.)* What if Paul not only publicly shamed Peter, but then strongly rejected his son as a fellow ministry partner?

Did you know that Peter wrote 1 and 2 Peter in the mid 60's AD just before he was crucified by Emperor Nero? Mark was certainly there when Peter wrote his letters *(Peter sent a greeting from him!)*, and he was very possibly/probably there when Peter died.

- Do you know that the Gospel of Mark was probably written about one year later? *(From Rome?)* What if John Mark watched Peter die and then said; "I have a job to do! I better get to writing."
- And how much of what Mark wrote in his Gospel was fed directly into his spiritual mind by Peter relating his own personal experiences with Jesus?

What I find so fascinating, amid all this conflict among early Christian leaders, is that the one guy that would not shut up, the guy who argued with everybody *(including Jesus)* about everything, the guy who had such a violent temper that he tried to slice off a guy's head in front of a squadron of soldiers – that guy became the Apostle of Peace!

> **1 Peter 3:8-9: "Finally, all of you should be of one mind. Sympathize with each other. Love each other as brothers and sisters. Be tenderhearted and keep a humble attitude. Don't repay evil for evil. Don't retaliate with insults when people insult you.**

**Instead, pay them back with a blessing. That is what God has called you to do, and he will grant you his blessing."** *(What?)*

Principle #4: If you have characteristics that are not Christ-like, do not use the excuse that "this is just who I am" – "people can like me or lump me"! If God can transform Peter from an angry, aggressive, violent Peter – to an Apostle of Peace – he can transform anybody! **1 Peter 3:10-11: "If you want to enjoy life and see many happy days, keep your tongue from speaking evil and your lips from telling lies. Turn away from evil and do good. Search for peace, and work to maintain it."** I say this with awe; Peter wrote that!

*One more event:* Stay with me here, this is not just a history lesson, it will fill in the gaps and lead us to the rest of Peter's amazing life. Remember the Jerusalem Council? What in the world were the Christian Jews to do with all those newly converted Gentiles? Should we make them all be circumcised? Should the Gentile Believers be forced to keep all 612 Old Testament laws? Paul and Barnabas take a "red-eye donkey train" into Jerusalem all hot and bothered. Peter comes back from wherever he has been ministering since Acts 12:

**Acts 15:6-11: "So the apostles and elders met together to resolve this issue. At the meeting, after a long discussion, Peter stood and addressed them as follows: "Brothers, you all know that God chose me from among you some time ago to preach to the**

**Gentiles so that they could hear the Good News and believe. God knows people's hearts, and he confirmed that he accepts Gentiles by giving them the Holy Spirit, just as he did to us. He made no distinction between us and them, for he cleansed their hearts through faith. So why are you now challenging God by burdening the Gentile believers with a yoke that neither we nor our ancestors were able to bear? We believe that we are all saved the same way, by the undeserved grace of the Lord Jesus."** *(Yes!)* Paul and Barnabas excitedly share about how Gentiles are flocking to faith in Jesus through their ministry, and then this:

**Acts 15:13-15,19: "When they had finished, James stood and said, 'Brothers, listen to me. Peter has told you about the time God first visited the Gentiles to take from them a people for himself. And this conversion of Gentiles is exactly what the prophets predicted.'... 'And so my judgment is..."**

And that is clearly that! James, Jesus' kid brother is now the undisputed head of the church in Jerusalem. Peter, the former leader, "is presented with a plaque and they all have punch and cupcakes." He fills out the application for an assisted living facility the new church has set up and signs up for Early Church Medicare. ☺ No he doesn't! As we have already noted, Peter is only in his mid-50's. He's going to live another 10-12 years before he is executed.

Principle #5: If God seems to elevate someone else and their talents and their spiritual gifts above your own, rejoice with them, bless them, and celebrate them. What God has for you as he develops your "maximum eternal impact" will have repercussions for generations to come.

- I can't help but believe that Peter had, at least, a passing question about James taking over his leadership spot, but in the end, James influences just the Jews around Jerusalem, and Peter's ministry spreads across the whole civilized world.
- Both write Epistles in the Bible. James writes one, it's a good one even though Martin Luther wanted it thrown out of the Canon. *(Works, not grace!)*
- Peter's two letters are pivotal to all of Christianity including giving us prophetic insight found nowhere else in Scripture!

I need to re-emphasize a point and then expand it: Peter didn't go to the Mediterranean and sail his new wind-powered yacht into the sunset. <u>He took off on his own missionary journeys</u>!

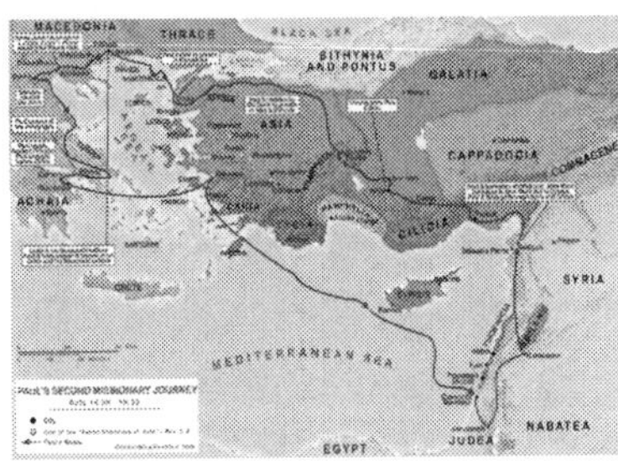


Everybody who has been around Christianity very long has seen these maps of Paul's missionary journeys. I love to draw word pictures in people's minds of what happened during the 2 ½ years Paul spent in Ephesus, or the 1 ½ years he spent in

Corinth. What we often don't think about is the fact that while Paul was taking his journeys as recorded in the book of Acts, Peter was taking missionary journeys of his own not recorded in the Bible much at all.

Besides the extra-biblical writings that allude to the above fact we do have Biblical clues that I want to show us. In the last chapter, in my effort to prove there was a Mrs. Peter, we looked at the fact that Jesus healed Peter's mother-in-law, certifying that at some point he had a wife – but even better were Paul's words to the Corinthian church:

> **1 Corinthians 9:4-5: "Don't we have the right to live in your homes and share your meals? Don't we have the right to bring a believing wife with us as the other apostles and the Lord's brothers do, and as Peter does?"**

So not only did Peter have a wife, his wife traveled with him in ministry! And if you happen to buy into the fact that John Mark was his son *(most certainly his spiritual son),* Mark may have traveled with his mom and dad *(spiritual?)* in the later years of their lives. But to where? Where were they traveling to? It looks like they may have arrived in Corinth at some point. *(based on the above)* but I found a couple other really amazing Biblical clues that lead us toward where this chapter needs to go. Paul in his earlier chats with the Corinthians in the same letter said this:

> **1 Corinthians 1:12-13: "Some of you are saying, "I am a follower of Paul." Others are saying, "I follow**

> **Apollos," or "I follow Peter," or "I follow only Christ." Has Christ been divided into factions? Was I, Paul, crucified for you? Were any of you baptized in the name of Paul? Of course not!"** Obviously Paul is writing this to make a different point, but don't miss the fact that some people in Corinth were saying they were "Peter followers"!

Why did the pagan gentile Corinthians care a whit about following Peter in Jerusalem 1,880 mile away? Because Peter wasn't 1,880 miles away! They knew him! They had met him *(and Mrs. Peter)* right there in their own city! They were so impressed by his first-hand stories about being with Jesus that some of the Corinthians said, "I'm not a follower of Paul, I am a follower of Peter!" But here is the icing on the cake: When Peter writes his first letter, who does he write it to?

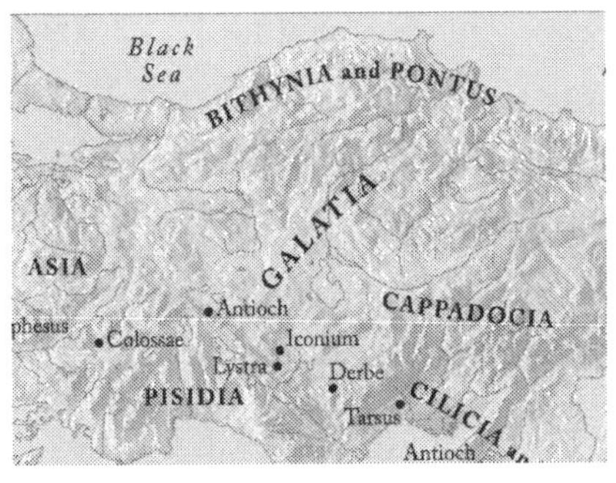


**1 Peter 1:1: "This letter is from Peter, an apostle of Jesus Christ. I am writing to God's chosen people who are living as foreigners in the provinces of Pontus, Galatia, Cappadocia, Asia, and Bithynia."**

Why is he addressing his letter specifically to them? Because he and Mrs. Peter had been there! These five provinces in Asia Minor *(modern day Turkey)* are where they had poured out their lives!

I could be wrong on this next point, but I don't think so. Paul was rather unknown. He probably didn't attract big crowds. Peter was another matter entirely. He had spent 800 plus hours of his life directly in the presence of Jesus!

This is the ruins of a first century theatre in Galatia. Can you not just see the local church announcing that Jesus' first disciple Peter, the Pentecost Preacher, the first great leader of the Jerusalem Church was coming to town? I doubt they could meet in a small stone church. They would have needed this amphitheatre. It's Peter, after all! He can tell us things Jesus said that nobody but him ever heard. *(Can't you imagine the Q and A session after his sermons?)*

It's fascinating to me that Paul's letter to the Galatians includes the section where Paul publicly tells Peter off. And get this: that <u>letter very probably arrived in Galatia while Peter and Mrs. Peter were teaching there</u>. The dates line up perfectly.

> Principle #6: Regardless of the opposition you face in life and ministry, lift your eyes off your circumstances and onto your Savior! Fix your eyes on Jesus, the Author and Finisher of your faith! Paul's letter to the Galatians has blessed millions/billions. Peter is just getting ready to pen the words of his first Epistle and

his letters will bless millions/ billions. Yet those two men were in conflict with one another. So, allow God to "maximize your eternal impact" regardless of the barriers *(human barriers)* you may run into on the journey!

- It is not impossible that it was Peter and Mrs. Peter's success in reaching people for Jesus' kingdom in Asia Minor that actually led to their persecution by the Roman Empire.
- By the time Peter pens his first words back to them, they are deep into the time when the 2nd Roman persecution *(the first really bad one)* is coming to a boil. And this is exactly the part of the Empire where the wildfires of persecution really started to burn.

**1 Peter 4:1-4: "So then, since Christ suffered physical pain, you must arm yourselves with the same attitude he had, and be ready to suffer, too. For if you have suffered physically for Christ, you have finished with sin. You won't spend the rest of your lives chasing your own desires, but you will be anxious to do the will of God. You have had enough in the past of the evil things that godless people enjoy—their immorality and lust, their feasting and drunkenness and wild parties, and their terrible worship of idols. Of course, your former friends are**

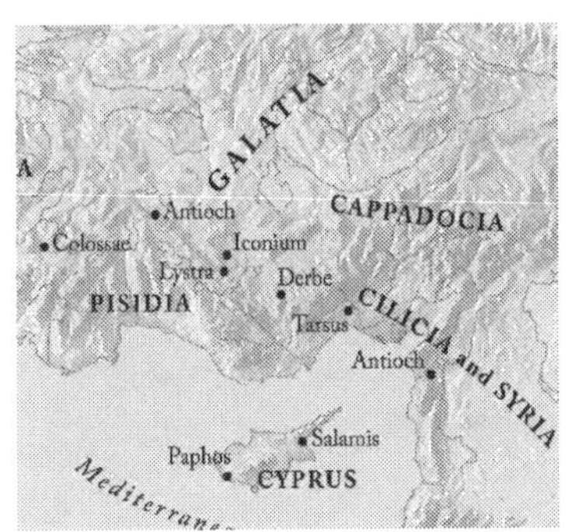

**surprised when you no longer plunge into the flood of wild and destructive things they do. So they slander you."**

Imagine living up in Cappadocia. Some of the people living there are persecuted Jewish Christians that fled from the persecution in Israel. But they are all preaching as they migrate and ten of thousands more are being saved. The new Cappadocian Believers are being saved right out of paganism. Suddenly, good friends living side by side are radically different people! They can't relate to the same things. The "immorality and lust and terrible worship of idols" that used to be considered a normal part of life is now being rejected by the Christians.

You might have had two members of the same family who have spent decades together, had sacrificed other humans as part of their worship together, had been involved in the most perverted kinds of sexual perversions all in the name of worship, and now suddenly one family says those practices are wrong, and sinful, and immoral.

"Civilized" society began to reject them wholesale and they were soon the outcasts. They *(as we said in the last chapter)* were considered "atheists" due to their denial of the existence and power of the Roman gods. Tacitus, *Roman historian and political analyst,* said their faith in Jesus "was not a real religion, but a deadly superstition"!

I honestly question if any of that was really the source of their outrage, they who worshipped hundreds of gods. I think they, like most others throughout history, were outraged that they were being told by the Christians that their perverted lifestyles were wrong and sinful and needed correction *(salvation).* By this time in Bithinya up by the Black Sea, just the rumor that you were a Christian would get you arrested, and if you didn't recant you would be executed. This was even before Nero burned Rome. This is before he blamed the fire on Christians that everybody was learning to hate. Peter writes back to them:

> **1 Peter 4:12-13, 19: "Dear friends, don't be surprised at the fiery trials you are going through, as if something strange were happening to you. Instead, be very glad—for these trials make you partners with Christ in his suffering, so that you will have the wonderful joy of seeing his glory when it is revealed to all the world... So if you are suffering in a manner that pleases God, keep on doing what is right, and trust your lives to the God who created you, for he will never fail you."**

We tend to think of "fiery trials" in light of somebody jumping in front of us at the grocery store or cutting us off on the interstate. But these people are thinking about "fiery trials" – if they claimed faith in Jesus they might/will be arrested and probably executed in front of their kids before the week was out!

But watch carefully – the idea of them possibly becoming "partners with Christ in his suffering" was not something they shrank back from. The idea of dying for their faith actually excited them! Can you imagine that? And the thought of dying on a cross, the Roman's most gruesome form of punishment – rather than recoiling from it, the early Believers longed for it, because that would most allow them to die like their Lord!

Peter knew he was going to die by crucifixion. Jesus had prophesied it. **John 21:18-19: "'...When you are old you will stretch out your hands, and someone else will dress you and lead you where you do not want to go.' Jesus said this to indicate the kind of death by which Peter would glorify God."** I wonder how differently I would live my life if I had a direct word from Jesus that my last breath would be breathed in anguish on a martyr's cross?

When Nero finally burns Rome he blames the Christians and hangs them on crosses along the Appian Way *(main street)* into Rome. Rather than shrinking from it, they each prayed like crazy they might be next. Peter was sure his cross was already being hewn from a local tree. It must have driven him to give everything toward "maximum eternal impact!"

Principle #7: We may never see that level of persecution *(or we might)*, but somehow God is calling us to the same kind of driving passion – allowing him to mold us into everything he designed us to be when he personally placed us on this planet!

# CHAPTER 6

# Chapter 7

*Peter's Humility and Martyrdom.*

---

We are going to come to the tumultuous end of Peter and Mrs. Peter's earthly life in this last chapter, but I want to drop back and show you a sequence of events that I've never quite caught before. Perhaps this is where Peter's real transformation initially begins, even before Jesus' death and resurrection. It certainly defines the end of his life.

- Before Peter's three denials and Jesus' private forgiving meeting with Peter after the resurrection.
- Before Jesus' dawn seaside meeting where he quizzes Peter, "Do you really love me?"
- Before the outpouring of the Holy Spirit on the day of Pentecost where Peter turns from an unlearned fisherman into a mighty life-changing preacher!

We watch these events unfold, and they are powerful. But back at the Last Supper we read something we might just ignore. We shouldn't! We alluded to this in chapter one, but not with this emphasis.

**John 13:1-5: "Before the Passover celebration, Jesus knew that his hour had come to leave this world and return to his Father. He had loved his disciples during his ministry on earth, and now <u>he showed</u>**

> **them the full extent of his love. It was time for supper, and the devil had already prompted Judas, son of Simon Iscariot, to betray Jesus. Jesus knew that the Father had given him authority over everything and that he had come from God and would return to God. So he got up from the table, took off his robe, wrapped a towel around his waist, and poured water into a basin. Then he began to wash the disciples' feet, drying them with the towel he had around him."**

When Jesus knew that satan had entered Judas to bring about his death on behalf of all humanity, he didn't jump up and scream at Judas, and warn the others they had a devil-filled person in their midst. Jesus' first response to finding out Judas had given himself over to satan was to get up, pick up a towel, and wash each of his disciple's feet including Judas!

*Jesus was combating pure evil with a towel of humility!*

He was preparing to face off with satan by humbling himself in front of the same sinful humans, he was going to die for. I often emphasize at the Last Supper, Jesus holding up the bread and wine saying, "This is my body broken for you. This is the new covenant in my blood." Perhaps I've imagined the washing of the disciple's feet as a disconnected side thought. What if it wasn't? What if the humble foot-washing was a major part in the defeat of sin and satan? Clearly, humility played a major role in our God becoming human.

> **Philippians 2:3, 5-9: "Don't be selfish; don't try to impress others. Be humble, thinking of others as better than yourselves...You must have the same attitude that Christ Jesus had. Though he was God, he did not think of equality with God as something to cling to. Instead, he emptied himself; he took the humble position of a servant and was born as a human being. When he appeared in human form, he humbled himself in obedience to God and died a criminal's death on a cross. Therefore, God elevated him to the place of highest honor and gave him the name above all other names."**

When Jesus heard that satan had entered Judas, "he took up a towel." Satan's strategic plan was to "conquer" Jesus by killing him on a cross, but he did not need to "conquer" him. Jesus **"humbled himself in obedience to God and died a criminal's death on a cross."** The devil was and is terrified of being defeated by the "towel of humility"! It's the "polar opposite" action, of why satan fell from Heaven. Satan's great sin was pride. He is the ultimate picture of arrogance. Not so oddly, that was the same sin that so defined Peter. But something brand new was starting to happen here:

> **John 13:6-7: "When Jesus came to Simon Peter, Peter said to him, "Lord, are you going to wash my feet?" Jesus replied, "You don't understand now what I am doing, but someday you will."** It won't be long until

you really start to catch on! You think I am kindly getting the road grime off your sandaled feet, but the fact is – I am defeating satan in the "Conflict of the Ages" and I am setting the stage for you to do so as well! *(Watch Peter's response.)*

**John 13:8: "No,' Peter protested, 'you will never ever wash my feet!' Jesus replied, 'Unless I wash you, you won't belong to me. You have** (ἔχω – echo, *to hold, possess)* **no part** (μέρος – meros – *portion or share*) **with me!'"**

Peter, if you are determined to continue on in your chronic arrogance, and aren't willing to learn what I am teaching you, then you might as well give up this "fishing for men" thing and go back to fishing for fish. **V. 9: Simon Peter exclaimed, 'Then wash my hands and head as well, Lord, not just my feet"!**

Perhaps that was the first real evidence that Peter was starting to make a turn! "I don't want to go back to fishing. I want to devote the rest of my life to being a follower of Jesus!" *Jesus responds,*

**John 13:10-12 MSG: "Jesus said, 'If you've had a bath in the morning, you only need your feet washed now and you're clean from head to toe.** (*My concern, you understand, is holiness, not hygiene.*) **So now you're clean. But not every one of you.' He knew who was betraying him. That's why he said, 'Not every one of you.'"** Jesus then finishes up his lesson on how to defeat satan's plans:

> **John 13:12-15 MSG: "Then he said, 'Do you understand what I have done to you?'** *(I'm not sure Jesus, I really am trying, Peter thinks, or says out loud.)* **You address me as 'Teacher' and 'Master,' and rightly so. That is what I am. If I the Master and Teacher, washed your feet, you must now wash each other's feet. I've laid down a pattern for you. What I've done, you do too. I'm only pointing out the obvious.'"**

Then Jesus launches into the longest and most profound private talk with his disciples in all of Scripture. They all get completely immersed in the new things he is telling them. He unfolds how Judas is going to betray him. When Peter balks, Jesus turns to him and prophesies that Peter will deny him three times before the rooster crows.

*"I go to prepare a place for you"! John 14:3*

He tells them he is indeed going to die, but that he will then go to Heaven to prepare a place for them, and he will come back to get them. He assures them: "**He is the Way, the Truth, and the Life**" *(John 14:6),* then he **promises the coming of the Holy Spirit who will lead them into all truth**! *(John 16:13)*

He promises them that they will be persecuted, and even martyred, but that the **Spirit of Truth will guide them** through it all. He tells them they will weep and grieve when he is finally taken away from them, but that it **is necessary that he leave, so that the Advocate, the Holy Spirit can come.** *(John 16:7)* He finishes with his High Priestly prayer to the Father, for his disciples. *(John 17:1-26)* Imagine them all listening intently *(including Peter – especially Peter)* as he hears Jesus say:

> **John 17:22-24: "I have given them the glory you gave me, so they may be one as we are one. I am in them and you are in me. May they experience such perfect unity that the world will know that you sent me and that you love them as much as you love me. Father, I want these whom you have given me to be with me where I am. Then they can see all the glory you gave me because you loved me even before the world began!"**

Imagine them all huddled around after Jesus finishes, muttering to each other, "Wow, what we just heard in the last 30 minutes literally sets the course for the rest of our lives." They're now beginning to understand:

1) <u>That</u> Jesus has to die! It was part of God's plan!

2) <u>Why</u> Jesus has to die! To wash and cleanse our sins, and the sins of the whole world!

3) The fact that <u>after his death he will leave earth to prepare their/our future home</u>.

4) The fact that <u>Jesus had to leave so the Spirit could come</u>, so that God's presence would not be limited to just where Jesus was/is.

5) The fact that <u>Jesus would/will not be gone forever</u>. <u>He will return</u> to take us to the place he is preparing for us.

Those disciples, their brains stuffed full of new information about their future, leave the Passover room and make their way out to the Garden of Gethsemane. The High Priest, the religious leaders, along with their private army, show up and confront Jesus just like he had prophesied. *(He has laid out the sequence of events a total of four times thus far. Peter heard every one of them!)*

The soldiers set out to arrest Jesus and lead him toward a trial just like Jesus had prophesied. They have every intention of killing him, just like Jesus prophesied. Peter whips out his sword and cuts off the ear of Malchus, the servant of the High Priest. And Jesus responds with something like *(and I paraphrase)* "What in the world are you doing"?

> **John 18:11: " Jesus said to Peter, 'Put your sword back into its sheath. Shall I not drink from the cup of suffering the Father has given me?'"** *(Which I already carefully explained to you!)* Do you not remember, just last evening when I fought the devil inside Judas by picking up a towel and washing his feet? I went low when the devil tried to go high. "It's my humility principle – You go all the way down, to get to the top"!

*The towel is mightier than the sword!*

When will you understand, Peter, that the towel is mightier than the sword? **"If you live by the sword, you will die by the sword"!** If you live by the towel – your life will exceed all your expectations!

As we noticed, it still took three denials and Peter "weeping bitterly." It took a private post-resurrection meeting with Jesus, a dawn seaside meeting with Jesus sitting across the fire asking Peter repeatedly: "Do you really, really love me"? As we have said for the last two chapters – we can measure the depth of transformation that takes place in Peter by reading what he would eventually write in his two Epistles:

> *Peter will write:* **1 Peter 5:1, 5-6: "And now, a word to you who are elders in the churches. I, too, am an elder and a witness to the sufferings of Christ. And I, too, will share in his glory when he is revealed to the whole world. All of you, dress yourselves in humility as you relate to one another, for 'God opposes the proud but gives grace to the humble.' So humble yourselves under the mighty power of God, and at the right time he will lift you up in honor."**

*Humble yourselves under the mighty hand of God!*

Watch how Peter ties humility to our own spiritual battle against the evil one in the very next verse. I've never noticed that these verses fall back to back.

> **1 Peter 5:8-10: "Stay alert! Watch out for your great enemy, the devil. He prowls around like a roaring lion, looking for someone to devour. Stand firm against him, and be strong in your faith. Remember that your family of believers all over the world is going through the same kind of suffering you are. In**

> **his kindness God <u>called you to share in his eternal glory by means of Christ Jesus. So after you have suffered a little while, he will restore,</u> support, and strengthen you, and he will place you on a firm foundation."**

Do we see the heart of Peter's new message? This so defines the huge transformations in Peter's soul: From slicing off Malchus' ear – defending Jesus from the very thing he said was going to happen the evening before – to being clothed in humility, fighting the evil one, sharing in Jesus' glory!

*Dress yourselves in humility as you relate to one another, for "God opposes the proud but gives grace to the humble."*

This may be the only place in the New Testament where we are told that our Savior *(who loves us so much that he died for us on a cross,)* "opposes" Believers. When we are prideful and arrogant – it's not that Jesus doesn't love us or is going to send us to hell. It is him saying, "I love you too much to leave you with the same inner attitude that caused satan to fall"!

I have become such a huge fan of Peter during the writing of this material, but for the first time I let myself have the thought: I wonder if Peter's sudden fall from visible leadership had something to do with a lack of humility, since "God opposes the proud but gives unusual grace to the humble!" *(I've often told younger pastors, "The moment you start believing the lauding people heap on you – you are in trouble"!)* Whatever the transfer from Peter's leadership to James involved, it included the transfer of a vital truth. Watch this from the pen of James:

> **James 4:5-9: "Do you think the Scriptures have no meaning? They say that God is passionate that the Spirit he has placed within us should be faithful to him. And he gives grace generously. As the Scriptures say, "God opposes the proud but gives grace to the humble." So humble yourselves before God. Resist the devil, and he will flee from you. Draw close to God, and God will draw close to you. Wash your hands, you sinners; purify your hearts, for your loyalty is divided between God and the world. Let there be tears for what you have done. Let there be sorrow and deep grief."** Isn't it interesting that the two New Testament writers who stress "God opposes the proud but gives grace to the humble," were Jerusalem church leader #1, Peter; and Jerusalem church leader #2, James? There has to be a back-story there, don't you think?

Thirty years later when Peter puts pen to paper, you can so hear his new mindset. His "preoccupation with Peter" goes away, and the "focus on his Savior, Jesus" comes sharply into the foreground!

> **1 Peter 1:18-20: "For you know that God paid a ransom to save you from the empty life you inherited from your ancestors. And it was not paid with mere gold or silver, which lose their value. It**

**was the precious blood of Christ, the sinless, spotless Lamb of God. God chose him as your ransom long before the world began, but now in these last days he has been revealed for your sake."**

**1 Peter 1:3-4: "All praise to God, the Father of our Lord Jesus Christ. It is by his great mercy that we have been born again because God raised Jesus Christ from the dead. Now we live with great expectation, and we have a priceless inheritance—an inheritance that is kept in heaven for you, pure and undefiled, beyond the reach of change and decay."**

Do you see the utter transformation in Peter? His chronic arrogance, his "in-grown eyeballs" always fixed on himself seem to be gone, and his attention is fixed like a laser on Jesus! And he seems determined to fix everyone else's eyes on Jesus too!

**11 Peter 1:13-16: "So prepare your minds for action and exercise self-control. Put all your hope in the gracious salvation that will come to you when Jesus Christ is revealed to the world. So you must live as God's obedient children. Don't slip back into your old ways of living to satisfy your own desires. You didn't know any better then. But now you must be holy in everything you do, just as God who chose you is holy. For the Scriptures say, 'You must be holy because I am holy.'"**

We looked closely at the geographical area of the churches that Peter was writing to. Just like when we read Paul's epistles we try to put ourselves inside the minds of the readers, the same is true for Peter's epistles. And we know exactly who Peter's initial readers were, and what was happening around them.

> **1 Peter 1:1: "This letter is from Peter, an apostle of Jesus Christ. I am writing to God's chosen people who are living as foreigners in the provinces of Pontus, Galatia, Cappadocia, Asia, and Bithynia."**

In the last 10 years of Peter's life this area that he is ministering to becomes a bull's-eye of Roman persecution. Peter and Mrs. Peter are traveling through this area, ministering in this area, making deep friendships in this area, but life has become very dangerous.

### *Mad Emperor Nero – has come into power!*

Nero was certifiably nuts! I told you that his mother murdered his step-father so he could rule at age 17. He then stabbed his mother to death, had his wife Octavia beheaded, and personally kicked his pregnant mistress Poppaea to death. He then forced the Roman Senate to make public offerings to the gods – for his restoration of "public morality." *(Like I said, he was certifiably nuts!)*

This is the very period of time when Peter with his eyes off of himself, and firmly onto his Savior and the growing Christian church that "Jesus is building," is writing to his many friends to strengthen their faith in the midst of growing persecution, and almost certain martyrdom.

**1 Peter 4:12-13: "Dear friends, don't be surprised at the fiery trials you are going through, as if something strange were happening to you. Instead, be very glad—for <u>these trials make you partners with Christ in his suffering</u>, so that you will have the wonderful joy of seeing his glory when it is revealed to all the world."**

And then he filled in the life lessons he had finally learned, **1 Peter 5:7-9: "Give all your worries and cares to God, for he cares about you. Stay alert! Watch out for your great enemy, the devil. He prowls around like a roaring lion, looking for someone to devour. Stand firm against him, and be strong in your faith."**

Transformed Peter, rather than running away from trouble, runs straight toward it. He settles in Rome for the last few years of his life. He begins to pour all the spiritual wisdom he has learned into his final letters. John Mark we saw last chapter was with him near and at the end. John Mark writes the Gospel of Mark *(the first gospel to be written)* from Rome one year later.

Here's what happened: On July 19, AD 64, a huge fire broke out in Rome. Of the 14 quarters in the city, only four escaped damage. Emperor Nero was rumored to have started the fire so that he could rebuild the poorer sections of town into his new dream city. To distract attention from himself he immediately put the blame on the Christians. Remember, the Christians had become increasingly disliked because they would not worship the Roman gods, and they would not take part in the perverted "acts of worship." It was strategic for Mad Nero to blame them because he got off scot-free and the Roman people's anger burned against the Christians.

- Peter and Mrs. Peter were right there! They were somewhere huddled outside the burning city as the fire raged.
- Peter may have been grabbing up copies of his newest letter, *(2 Peter)* to keep them from the flames.
- Within days Christians were being burned on crosses for the horrible fire they had nothing to do with.
- Peter and Mrs. Peter get caught up in the chaotic aftermath and are arrested.
- Peter knew exactly what was coming for him. How did he know? Because Jesus had told him 30 years earlier.

**John 21:18-19: "'I tell you the truth, when you were young, you were able to do as you liked; you dressed yourself and went wherever you wanted to go. But when you are old, you will stretch out your hands, and others will dress you and take you where you don't want to go.' Jesus said this <u>to let him know by what kind of death he would glorify God</u>."**

So Peter has his mind locked onto what was coming for him, he doesn't run from it. He was the one writing to others that persecution and martyrdom were simply "taking part in the sufferings of Jesus." What is a little odder to me is that he took Mrs. Peter with him to Rome. If he had a strong suspicion that he was going to be crucified, why not tuck his wife away somewhere to keep her safe? My guess is, she wouldn't let him!

She was clearly a spiritual giant of a woman! She had been stomping all over the Empire evangelizing pagans beside her husband. Mr. Peter may very well have offered Mrs. Peter a pathway out of the finale, and she might have responded, "I know exactly why you are headed into Rome, and I intend to be right beside you when Jesus' prophesy is fulfilled! And she apparently was. Her arrest alongside Peter is not mentioned in the Bible, but it sure is part of historical tradition.

> *Clement of Alexandria, an early Christian theologian records:* "**They say, accordingly, that Peter, on seeing his wife led to death, rejoiced on account of her call and conveyance home, and called very encouragingly and comfortingly, addressing her by name, "Remember the Lord." Such was the marriage of their blessed and perfect disposition towards those dearest to them."** *(Clement, The Stromata, Book VII.)* Eusebius – the bishop of Caesarea picks up the same story in his Church History:

Peter not only brought his wife to Rome at the most hideous of times. He watched her get arrested and then he watched her die! The amazing thing to me is that the man who put his own wants and wishes ahead of anything and everything was now totally sold out to putting Jesus and his kingdom first! *(Including watching the martyrdom of his own beloved wife!)*

Peter didn't have long, before he joined his wife in Heaven.

Another famous Clement, Clement of Rome the first Bishop of Rome *(not Peter!)* from right there in the capital a handful of years after Peter's death wrote:

> **"Peter, who by reason of wicked jealousy** ***(of pagans),*** **not only once or twice but frequently endured suffering and thus, bearing his witness, went to the glorious place which he merited." (5:4)**
> the *Letter to the Corinthians* (c. 96 ce; 5:1–6:4)

The stunning part in all of this – Is that the arrogance, the pride of Peter has been totally replaced by humility. His constant self-centeredness had been replaced by others-centeredness. His humility has increasingly taught him how to resist the devil.

The spiritual defensive against the forces of evil and the spiritual offensive for the forces of God, in this world were/are directly linked to his/our willingness to lay down pride, and pick up Jesus' humility!

# ACKNOWLEDGEMENTS

God nudged **Cass Everett**, after her retirement from the business world, to sell her home in Pennsylvania and move to the 'unknown land' of South Florida. In God's providential plan she ended up just a few miles from our church. Cass' use of her spiritual gifts has become invaluable at Grace Emmanuel Church, but she has become, to me, a gift from God.

Who, but God, could have planned an ADD pastor linking up with a gentle "do it by the book" editor. This book literally would not have been in print without the time Cass has invested in it.

She has poured so, so many long hours into repeatedly editing and reviewing and re-editing the manuscript for this book and *"Unmasking Revelation, Spiritual Warfare, Heaven, and Jonah."* No one but God will ever know the long evenings she sat up late into the night finding the phrase that didn't quite communicate, finding the exclamation mark before the quotation mark rather than after it, finding the underline extending under the period. Cass' amazing attention to detail will be a legacy that outlasts both of our lives!

**Penny Worley**, the administrative secretary at Grace Emmanuel Church, designed the cover of this book. She is also a special gift from God in my life. In spite of the already huge demands on her time at the church, when I walk into Penny's office with a personal project, she never fails to give away her time, and always with excellence beyond measure.

A special thanks to **Holly Jochum** and **Helen Rhoades** for their "beta" reading and editing of the manuscript.

A big thank you to **Tom VanDuyne** for his astounding likeness to Peter in the pictures throughout this book.

Another big thank you to **Elijah Brogan** for his photography skills in taking the "Peter" pictures.

# SCRIPTURE BY BOOK INDEX

# SCRIPTURE BY CHAPTER INDEX

## ADDITIONAL SCRIPTURE VERSIONS USED

# ABOUT THE AUTHOR

Sam Chess has served as a Pastor on the Treasure Coast of Florida, for more than 40 years. He serves as the Senior Pastor of Grace Emmanuel Church *(EFCA)* in Port Saint Lucie. *(graceemmanuel.com)* He and his wife Sue founded the church in 1990.

Grace Emmanuel has two radio programs called "GRACE ALIVE" on the 100,000 watt regional Christian radio station WCNO. *(WCNO.com)* The four times a week program reaches from Miami to Melbourne, FL, across much of the state, and into the Bahamas.

Sam serves on the board of the Treasure Coast Christian Alliance, which seeks to align government officials, business leaders, and Church leaders in unity and purpose.

Sam and Sue have three children and eight wonderful grandchildren. Sue Chess serves as the Executive Director of Care Net Pregnancy Services of the Treasure Coast.

Sam holds a Bachelor's degree from the Hobe Sound Bible College and a Master's degree from Trinity International University.

Sam is also the author of four other books, **Unmasking Revelation**, (2020) **Spiritual Warfare,** (2022) **Heaven,** (2023) and **Jonah** (2023).

*Contact Sam at samchess.com , or text Sam at 772.528.9127*

# OTHER BOOKS BY SAM CHESS

**JONAH (2023)**

Generations of Sunday School children have heard the story of Jonah. It's the story "about a big fish swallowing a man and the then spitting him back out onto dry land."

Actually the word "fish' is only mentioned four times in the whole book! Clearly, the point of the story must be about far more than "a fish swallowing a man." The fish is mentioned just 4 times. Jonah is mentioned 18 times, God is mentioned 38 times!

It turns out that Jonah is not the hero of the story. GOD IS! The book is actually about God's extraordinary, unstoppable, GRACE, even toward the sons and daughters who choose to run away from him!

When our Heavenly Father holds open His arms of invitation, we know that the prodigal son or daughter sometimes runs in the opposite direction! Jonah did! Perhaps that describes some of us reading these words. But the amazing story about Jonah is that God's love never gives up. God's grace always pursues us! HIs outstretched arms reach out to us, even in the fog of our deepest sins!

God's grace is a powerful, unstoppable, unmerited river

pouring in our direction. But it is not always easy to accept, not easy to even believe in, not easy to receive. In this "JONAH" book, Sam Chess helps us to experience the consistent, ever-faithful, relentless, constantly-pursuing, unrestrained, love and grace of God reaching into each of our lives.

**SPIRITUAL WARFARE** (2023)

In Spiritual Warfare, Sam Chess shows us that Jesus left Heaven and came into this world as a savior, as OUR savior, to forgive and cleanse our sins! But Jesus also came into this world as a HEAVENLY WARRIOR to do fatal damage to satan's "kingdom of darkness".

Jesus didn't come to this earth to have a word spat with satan. He came to destroy him! Jesus didn't just come to save us from sin - He came to save us from satan!

What you see and hear from demons when they come in contact with Jesus and scream out in fear in the Gospels should make you never fear them again in your life! The truth is - demons are scared to death of your God, they are scared to death of your savior, and they are scared to death of YOU, a Redeemed Saint, and the presence of God that lives in you.

They know something that they hope that you never find out: They know that all the power is on your side? You are a Son or Daughter of the Most Hight God! And they are scared to death of what you will do with your life when you figure that out!

**<u>HEAVEN</u>** (2023)

If I were to ask each of us where we will be one minute after we breathe our last breath, most of us would respond – I'll be in Heaven! Good! So where is that? What is it like there? What will you be doing? Many people might form their response from a modern book about somebody who said they died and visited Heaven – but we all should really be asking, "What does the Bible actually say"?

Many people have the misconception that the Bible is vague on the subject. The truth is the word "Heaven" shows up 913 times from the earliest pages of Scripture to its description in the last three sentences, along with hundreds of additional passages that describe Heaven without actually using the word.

What if we could organize all that Biblical information to be able to gaze right inside of Heaven, be able to see exactly where our saintly relatives are, and start to form a mental picture of what they are doing right now – and what we will be doing for all of eternity?

We all say we're looking forward to the "no more pain and tears" part. That's good! When we do finally find ourselves in Heaven and the curse of sin has fallen away, and the pain, and the fears, and the confusion of this sin-soaked life have faded from view... When we for the first time walk into the Throne Room of God – and from deep in our soul, a praise begins to rise joining in unison with millions of other "Saints" and millions of angels, worshipping in ways we only get the briefest glimpse of now – all the traumas of this life will suddenly seem worthwhile!

But what if that is just the beginning? What if there is far more to Heaven? What if what we are learning and experiencing in this life is just preparing us for what the book of Romans calls being "heirs of God and co-heirs with Christ"?

What in the world could Apostles John and Paul have possibly meant when they describe us as eternally "reigning" with Christ? It's all in here – let's dig it out!

**UNMASKING REVELATION** (2019)

The Book of Revelation was never meant to produce fear, it was always meant to ignite awe and worship.

There is a special blessing promised to all who read and obey the words of Revelation (1:3). Yet many Christians slam their Bible shut before reading because they find the end times prophecy to be confusing, weird, and even scary.

Revelation was never meant to be ignored or skipped over. To the Early Church it was the most exciting thing they had ever read! In *Unmasking Revelation,* Sam Chess walks through how Jesus purposely left first century Christians with the vivid hope of His return, and how the letter of Revelation was given as a careful guide to how it all would end. Jesus was going to victoriously win and satan, and death, and hell, and even the curse of sin itself (22:3) would be purged off this planet!

In *Unmasking Revelation,* Sam had intentionally made the difficult parts of Revelation understandable, and the weird and frightening parts are "unmasked" to simply unfold the chronological storyline of Jesus' *(and we Believers)* final triumphant victory over satan and sin and evil.

**If you liked this book, please leave a review on Amazon.com**

1) Go to Amazon.com

2) Find “Peter” by Sam Chess

3) Scroll down to “customer reviews”

4) Select “write a customer review”

5) Write a short review of the book

6) Select the number of stars you think the book is worth

Made in the USA
Columbia, SC
13 November 2024